Introduction

The "Five Hundred Bible Subjects" which appear outlined in the following pages, have been gathered from the Sacred Word and used during the last thirty years in various ways, while seeking to help others in the things of God. For the most part, they have been used in giving Bible Readings, Simple Addresses, and Homely Talks to companies of young believers and others, who needed the Bread of Life broken small, and the Truth ministered in words easy to be understood by the common people.

They are chiefly Outlines and Groupings of Fundamental Truths and Elementary Doctrines of the Faith, upon which the confidence and hope of children of God in all ages has reposed, and by feeding upon which, spiritual life is developed, spiritual health maintained, and spiritual strength derived for walk and service.

They recall many happy seasons, when under the guidance of the Spirit, the Word was opened for the renewing, refreshing and strengthening of the inner man, and for instruction, enlightenment and guidance in the path marked out in the Word for the saints to tread.

They have been used for searching, meditation and ministry amid companies gathered around the family board: in the highland farmhouse: in the miner's cot, with its glowing fire: in the dainty parlor, where in homely style, and after a cup of tea had been handed round, "The Book" was brought out to provide the evening's fare. By these and other such informal means, as surely as though the stated and wholesome public ministry of the Truth, the Words of the Lord are brought into everyday use, and form the subjects of consideration and of conversation in daily life, talking of them while sitting in the house, and walking by the way (Deut. vi. 7). Thus the lambs and sheep of the Lord's ransomed flock are led to and fed in "the green pastures" and beside "the quiet waters"; the trees of the Lord are kept "full of sap" and bear their "fruit in due season," and the church, to which the living Lord and Head in heaven still ministers of His fullness, in the Spirit, through the Word, is sanctified and edified.

With the earnest desire and fervent prayer that these Subjects and Outlines may be made serviceable to others who seek, amid common joys and sorrows, to feed the lambs and strengthen the feeble ones of the Lord's flock, they are here passed on, with a deep sense of their imperfection, to all who in every place call upon the Name, meditate upon the word, and serve the Lord Jesus.

KILMARNOCK, JAN. 1ST, 1905.   J. R.

FIVE HUNDRED
BIBLE SUBJECTS

WITH

SUGGESTIVE OUTLINES AND NOTES.

FOR

BIBLE STUDENTS,
PREACHERS AND TEACHERS.

By
John Ritchie

ISBN 0-88019-301-8

Schmul Publishing Co., Inc.
Wesleyan Book Club   1993   Salem, Ohio

Copyright © 1993
by Schmul Publishing Co.

Printed by
Old Paths Tract Society, Inc.
Shoals, Ind. 47581

Index

Contents

THE WORD OF GOD;

HINTS ON ITS READING AND STUDY.

The Bible is God's own Book, His Divine and perfect Revelation, His living Voice speaking unto men, in all ages. It should be read prayerfully, listened to reverently, received believingly, obeyed implicitly. Its central object is Christ, its Teacher the Holy Spirit, its design man's blessing, its end the glory of God. It is the instrument in regeneration, the means of sanctification, the channel of edification to the believer. It gives light upon all his path, regulates all his relationships and gives counsel for all his behavior, in the family, the church, and the world. It should be dealt with daily, personally, prayerfully, perseveringly, in the presence of God, for the soul's individual need. It is bread to feed, light to search, water to cleanse; the secret of growth, the source of strength, the shield of preservation, the sword of victory. *Read* it regularly, connectedly, consecutively. Give your heart and mind the whole field of Scripture; Christ in type and prophecy in the Old; Christ on earth, in life, in death and in glory, in the New. The Bible is from God. It is Divinely inspired, has been miraculously guarded, is of supreme authority, all-sufficient, eternal. The standard of doctrine, the channel of blessing, the rule of life, the final appeal on all God's things, in all ages. Nothing needs to be added to it because nothing is awanting; nothing taken from it, because nothing is superfluous. Like its Author, it is Divine, unchanging, eternal. Its writers were men, but their words were the words of the Holy Spirit (2 Pet. i. 21; 2 Sam. xxiii. 2). It was accepted as it existed, was read, used and spoke of as "the Word of God" (Mark vii. 13), "the Scripture" which cannot be broken (John x. 35) by the Lord Jesus, of whom it is declared that he "knew all men" (John ii. 24), and had "all things" given into His hand (John iii. 35), of whom His own disciples confessed, "Now are we sure that thou knowest all things" (John xvi. 30)—a glory which some deny Him. Would He have put His imprimature upon a book, accepting its various divisions as they stood (Luke xxiv. 43-44), calling it the "Scriptures," opening His disciples' understanding that they might understand these Scriptures, and sending the Spirit to teach and guide them into "all the truth" therein contained, had He believed, as some now would fain persuade us, that the Book is a combination of truth and error, of Divine revelation and human legend? The Bible carries its own credentials. It causes its voice to be heard. Its light convicts, its warnings alarm, its grace converts the soul. It shows man, reveals God, testifies of Christ. It is the instrument in conversion, the means of instruction, the power for edification. It teaches the babe, guides the youth, and fully furnishes "the man of God" unto all good works. All God's mighty men have been readers, students, lovers of the Book. Charles H. Spurgeon says: "The Word, the simple, pure, infallible Word of God we must live upon, if we are to become strong against error and tenacious of truth." Robert C. Chapman writes: "Meditation on the Word of God is the chief means of our growth in grace. It is a thriving soul that finds the Book of God growing more and more precious." J. Nelson Darby testifies—"My joy, my comfort, my food, my strength for near thirty years have been, the Scriptures received implicitly as the Word of God. In the beginning of that period I was put through the deepest exercise on that point. Did heaven and earth, the visible church, and man himself, crumble into nonentity, I should, through grace since that epoch, hold to the Word as an unbreakable link between my soul and God."

Read the Word *daily*. Set apart a fixed time for the daily reading of the Word. When left to be read at any time it is frequently not read at all. Keep to your set time, do not allow trivial engagements, social functions, or business calls to deprive you of it. God and the soul first, other things fall into their proper places after.

Read the Word *prayerfully*. In prayer you speak to God: through the Word God speaks to you. While your eyes rest on the sacred page, let your heart be lifted up to God, with the prayer that the eye of faith may be opened to "behold wondrous things" out of His law (Psa. cxix. 18). Remember that the Spirit of God is your Teacher, that He by whose inspiration these words of God were written, alone can unfold their spiritual meaning to your understanding and your heart (I Cor. ii. 10-14), and make them strength and comfort to your soul. When you discover some fresh aspect of truth, when you dig out some hitherto unknown treasure, when some new ray of heaven's light enters your heart, meditate on it, speak to God about it, praise Him for it, ask Him to make it your soul's personal possession, to make it good to you experimentally.

George Müller, of Bristol, says: "It is a common temptation of Satan, to make us give up the reading of the Word and prayer when our enjoyment is gone, as if it were of no use to read the Scriptures when we do not enjoy them, and as if it were of no use to pray when we have no spirit of prayer; whilst the truth is, in order to enjoy the Word, we ought to continue to read it, and the way to obtain a spirit of prayer is, to continue praying, for the less we read the Word of God, the less we desire to read it, and the less we pray, the less we desire to pray."

HELPS to the study of the Bible are not to be despised, nor ought they to be neglected. We may surely profit through the toils of others who have given their time and talents to the textual criticism, careful translation, and microscopic examination of the Sacred word, and thus, according to the will of God, His servants become helpers one of another. But let the Book of books, the inspired, eternal Word of the living God have the chief and honored place. Let it be THE Book, the supreme authority, and all else but as helps to the discovery of its holy treasures, hewers of wood and drawers of water to the sacred volume which they seek to serve. Have a good REFERENCE BIBLE, with readable type and margin sufficient for notes and jottings; one good enough to last a number of years of hard wear, for it is not good to change your Bible often. A *fac-simile* Bible, the same in all sizes, in which you will soon learn to find the verses by their location and always in the same place, whether large or small in type. A Revised or other TRANSLATION, a complete and trustworthy CONCORDANCE to the Bible, and a reliable BIBLE DICTIONARY are useful and now easily acquired helps in the study of the Sacred Word. These with EXPOSITIONS of truths by gifted and Divinely-taught ministers of the Word, are to be received with thanksgiving and used with wisdom, always in leading you to the Word to dig there for yourselves, never to take its place, or to be read as a lesson book to be repeated to others, without having been proved or personally experienced in your own souls. COMMENTARIES, as a rule, are theological and dry; many of them muddy, some quite erroneous, and generally even when sound, cold-blooded, with little in them to enrich the soul, exercise the conscience, or lead the heart out to God. The Word of God itself, under the teaching of the Spirit, opens its secret treasures to the waiting heart, which in patient, diligent, and continuous study of its sacred pages, seeks to become acquainted with the will of God to do it, and with the ways of the Lord to walk in them. Regular and systematic study of the Word, day by day, and every day, gathering here a little and there a little, treasuring, husbanding and using what we gather, is the slow but sure and only way of becoming acquainted with the whole truth of God.

METHODS of study must be largely left to the tastes, the capabilities, and the conveniences of the individual. What suits one well does not lend itself to another. Clearly there must be some method, or many methods adopted; random reading profits little. The Word should be studied systematically, consecutively, topically. The character, scope, subject, and purpose of a book, the outlines, context, setting of a Psalm; the subject, occasion, date, and key words of an Epistle sought for and grasped; then its teaching will be understood, its doctrinal, dispensational, and practical parts distinguished, and its application made plain; "rightly dividing the Word of truth" (2 Tim. ii. 16), as the apostle commands. Error is often truth distorted, wrenched from its connection, and presented from one side apart from the countertruth needed for its balance.

SEARCHING the Scriptures, tracing a word, a subject through them, as a dog scents (for such is the meaning of the word "search the scriptures" in John v. 39), is one method. "Searching the Scriptures"—examining them closely, scrutinizing and comparing them, as the Bereans did (Acts xvii. 12), is equally important for the accurate study of the Word. Thus acquainted with the truths of Scripture, having them dwelling richly in the mind and heart, kept there in freshness by the Holy Spirit who indwells the saint (2 Tim. i. 13-14), they will be brought to remembrance, and wisdom given to utter them by that same Spirit (1 Cor. ii. 13-14), in due season with blessing to others. May the Book of God, the Written word, in which the Living Word is unveiled, become increasingly precious unto and be unceasingly used by all the people of God.

> "A glory gilds the Sacred page,
>   Majestic like the sun;
> It gives a light to every age,
>   It gives, but borrows none."

FOUNDATION TRUTHS
OF THE GOSPEL

1. Regeneration.

A New Life from God, An Inward Working in the Soul.

Its Necessity (John iii. 7; Gal. vi. 15; Eph. ii. 2).
Its Nature (John iii. 5; 2 Cor. v. 17; Eph. ii. 10, iv. 24).
Its Agent (John iii. 8, vi. 63; 2 Cor. iii. 6; Titus iii. 5).
Its Instrument (1 Pet. i. 23; James i. 18; John v. 24).
Its Means (1 John v. 1; Gal. iii. 26; John i. 12-13).
Its Fruits (1 John iii. 9; Rom. vi. 22; 1 John iii. 10).
Its Manifestation (1 John v. 1-2; 1 John iii. 16).

2. Conversion.

A New Attitude Toward God, an Outward Change in the Life.

The Need (Matt. xviii. 3; Acts iii. 19; Isa. liii. 6).
The Act (1 Thess. 1. 9; 1 Pet. ii. 24; Acts xxvi. 18).
The Motive (Acts xi. 21; Hosea xiv. 8; Phil. iii. 8).
The Hindrances (Acts xxviii. 27, xiii. 8; John vi. 66).

3. Justification.

A New State Before God, a Forensic Term.

The Sinner's State (Rom. iii. 10; Isa. lxiv. 6; Rom. iii. 9).
God, the Justifier (Rom. viii. 33, iv. 25).
Christ's Death the Procuring Cause (1 Pet. iii. 18).
Grace the Spring (Rom. iii. 24; Gal. ii. 16-24).
Faith the Principle (Rom. v. 1; Acts xiii. 39).
Resurrection the Witness (Rom. iv. 25, v. 18).
Works the Evidence (James ii. 26; Titus iii. 8).

4.   Redemption.

The Word means "to buy back" and set free.
There is a Redemption by Blood and by Power.

Man's Ruin (Isa. lii. 3; John viii. 34; Rom. vi. 20).
Man's Helplessness (Psa. xlix. 7; Micah vi. 7).
A Redeemer Provided (Job xxxiii. 24; Psa. cxi. 9).
Redemption by Blood (Eph. i. 7; Acts xx. 28; Heb. ix. 12).
Redemption by Power (Eph. i. 13-14, iv. 30; Rom. viii. 23).
Redemption from Iniquity (Titus ii. 14; 1 Pet. i. 18).
Redemption from the Curse (Gal. iii. 13; Psa. ciii. 4).
Redemption of the Body (Rom. viii. 23; Phil. iii. 20 R.V.).

5.   Salvation.

Threefold—Past, Present, Future.

Past—From Sin's Penalty (Rom. i. 16; Acts xxviii. 18; Acts xvi. 31; Rom. x. 10; 1 Cor. xv. 2; 2 Tim. i. 9).
Present—From Sin's Power (Heb. vii. 25; Rom. v. 9; James i. 23; 1 Tim. iv. 6; Phil. ii. 12).
Future—From Sin's Presence (Rom. xiii. 11; Heb. ix. 28; Phil. iii. 20; 1 Thess. v. 8).
The First is immediate, Secured by Christ's Death.
The Second is continuous by Christ's Life.
The Third is prospective at Christ's Coming.

6.   Judgment

In Various Aspects.

Judgment of the Sinner, Predicted (Heb. ix. 27; Eccl. xi. 9; 2 Pet. ii. 2-4; Heb. x. 27).
Judgment of the Believer, Past (John v. 24 R.V.; Rom. viii. 1, viii. 23-24; Gal. ii. 20).
Judgment of the Servant, Future (2 Cor. v. 10; Rev. xxii. 12; Col. iii. 24-25; 1 Cor. iv. 1-5).

There is no such thing as a General Judgment taught in Scripture.

7. Sanctification.

The word means "to set apart," "to separate."

The Sanctification of Believers (1 Cor. i. 2; 2 Thess. ii. 13; 1 Pet. i. 3).

1. Perfect and Once for All—The Work of the Cross, the Result of the Sacrifice of Christ (1 Cor. vi. 11; Acts 22. 32, xxvi. 18; Heb. ii. 11).

2. Progressive and Continuous—The Work of the Spirit through the Word in the believer (1 Thess. v. 23; John xvii. 17).

Types and Illustrations—The Sabbath sanctified (Gen. ii. 3); the First-Born "set apart" (Exod. xiii. 2); The Brazen Altar, the Holy Garments (Exod. xxix. 44, xxviii. 2) and the Holy Mount (2 Pet. i. 18) accounted "sacred" or "holy," not intrinsically, but "set apart" by the presence and for the service of God.

8. Perfection.

The words "Perfect" and "Perfection" represent several Greek words having different meanings.

1. *Teleois,* meaning "Accomplished, Complete," which occurs in Matthew v. 48 as applied to God, in Rom. x. 2 to His "will," in 1 John iv. 17 to His love, and is rendered "full age" in Heb. v. 14, "full grown" in Heb. v. 14 R.V.

2. *Pleero,* meaning "full," rendered "Perfect" in Rev. iii. 2; "complete," Col. iii. 10; and "full" in 1 John i. 4.

3. *Katarizo,* meaning "thoroughly adjusted," as in "mending nets" (Mark i. 19). It is translated "perfectly joined together" (1 Cor. i. 10); "restore" (Gal. vi. 1). By carefully distinguishing these words many of the difficulties regarding this subject are removed.

Absolutely, Perfection is in God alone (Job i. 8; Psa. xxxvii. 16).

Relatively, it is said to be of men (Job i. 18; Psa. xxxvi. 17).

1. Perfection of God (Matt. v. 48; Rom. xii. 2; 2 Sam. xxiii. 11).
2. Perfection of Christ (Heb. ii. 10; xii. 2, R.V.).
3. Perfect Sacrifice (Heb. x. 11-14, vii. 28).
4. Perfect Conscience (Heb. x. 2-14; John xvii. 10).
5. Perfection in Practice (Matt. v. 48; 2 Cor. xiii. 11).
6. Perfection in Growth (Heb. v. 14; Phil. iii. 15).

"Sinlessness," "perfection" of the creature, is an error (see 1 John i. 8).

9. Assurance.

Certainty, not Doubt, is the Christian's normal condition.

What Believers *Are* (1 Cor. i. 18; 1 John ii. 12).
What Believers *Know* (1 John iii. 14, v. 19, iii. 24, v. 11).
What Believers *Have* (Eph. i. 7, v. 1; John iii. 14).
What Believers *Expect* (1 John iii. 2; 1 Thess. iv. 16).

10. Sonship.

The word *Teknon* means "begotten ones," and occurs in John i. 12, xi. 52; Rom. viii. 16-17; Phil. ii. 15; 1 John iii. 1-2.
The word *Whyos* means "sons," and occurs in Gal. iii. 26, iv. 6-7; Rom. viii. 14-19; Heb. xii. 5-7-8.
The Origin of Sonship (Gal. iii. 26; 1 John v. 1).
The Spirit of Sonship (Gal. iv. 6-7; Rom. viii. 14).
The Place of Sonship (John viii. 35; Gal. iv. 5).
The Manifestation of Sonship (Rom. viii. 19-29).

11. Rest.

There are at least three words translated "Rest" in the New Testament.

1. *Anapausis*—"an up rest," as in Matt. xi. 28.
2. *Katapausis*—"a down rest," as in Heb. iv. 4.
3. *Sabbatismos*—"a Sabbath rest," as in Heb. iv. 9.
Rest for the Sinner (Matt. xi. 28)—At the Cross.
Rest for the Saint (Matt. xi. 29)—In Subjection.
Rest in the Lord (Psa. xxxvi. 7)—In Confidence.
Rest with the Lord (2 Thess. i. 7)—In Glory.
Rest that Remains (Heb. iv. 9)—Eternal.

12.   Life.

The Sinner's State (Eph. ii. 1; Eph. iv. 18; John vi. 53).
The Source of Life (John v. 26; Psa. xxxvi. 9).
The Life Manifested (1 John i. 4; John i. 4).
The Life Laid Down (John x. 15; John xii. 24).
The Life Imparted (John x. 10, xx. 31; Rom. vi. 23).
The Life Possessed (John iii. 36; 1 John v. 12-13).
The Life Exhibited (2 Cor. iv. 10; Gal. ii. 20).
The Life in Fruition (Titus i. 2; Jude 21; Rom. vi. 22).

FUNDAMENTAL TRUTHS
OF THE FAITH

13. The Triune God.

(Read Matt. xxviii. 18; 2 Cor. xiii. 14.)

The Father (Eph. iv. 6; Rom. xi. 36; Rom. ix. 5).
The Son (John v. 20, x. 20, xvii. 5; Matt. xi. 27).
The Holy Spirit (John xiv. 26, xv. 26, xvi. 7).
Godhead ascribed to each (Rom. i. 20; Heb. i. 8).

14. Trinity Acting in Unity.

In Creation (Gen. i. 1, with John i. 4; Job xxvi. 13).
In Incarnation (John iii. 16; Heb. x. 5; Luke i. 35).
In Redemption (Heb. ix. 14; 1 Pet. iii. 18; Gal. ii. 20).
In Salvation (Luke xv. 4, 8, 22; Eph. i. 4, 7, 13).
In Communion (Eph. ii. 18; Rom. viii. 27; 2 Cor. xiii. 14).
In Glory (Rev. i. 4-5; Phil. iii. 21; Jude 23).

15. The Work of God the Father.

Election of the Saints (Eph. i. 3).
Giver of the Son (John iii. 16).
Author of Incarnation (Gal. iv. 4).
Anointing for Service (Acts x. 38).
Bruising in Death (Isa. liii. 6-11).
Active in Resurrection (Rom. vi. 4).
Sealer of Salvation (2 Cor. i. 21-22).

16. The Eternal Godhead.

The Eternal God (Deut. xxxiii. 27; Isa. lvii. 15).
The Eternal Son (John i. 1; Micah v. 2 margin).
The Eternal Spirit (Heb. ix. 14; Gen. i. 2; Job xxvi. 13).

17.   Three Great Truths

Concerning Christ in John, Chapter i., Verse 1.

His Eternity—"In the *beginning* was the Word."
His Personality—"The Word was *with* God."
His Divinity—"The Word *was* God."

18.   Son of God.

In the Eternal Past (John viii. 58, i. 30, xvii. 5).
As Given to the World (John iii. 16; Rom. viii. 3).
As Born of the Virgin (Luke i. 35; John i. 14).
As Owned of the Father (Matt. iii. 17; Luke ix. 35).
As Confessed by Men (Matt. xvi. 16; Acts ix. 20).
As Raised from the Dead (Rom. i. 4; Heb. i. 1).

19.   The Son of Man.

A Title only used by the Lord concerning Himself, never by His disciples in speaking to or of Him. It designates His true Manhood, as distinguished from the "sons of men," whose humanity is "fallen."

In Service and Suffering (Matt. xi. 19; Luke ix. 56).
Coming To Save (Luke xix. 10; John vi. 27).
Suffering unto Death (Luke ix. 22, xxiv. 7).
A Sacrifice for Sin (John iii. 14, xii. 34).
Risen from the Dead (Matt. xvii. 9, xii. 32).
Glorified in Heaven (Acts vii. 56; Rev. i. 13).
Coming in Judgment (Matt. xxiv. 17, xxv. 31).

20.   The Divine Sonship of Christ:

A Sevenfold Testimony.

Jesus proclaimed it (Matt. xxvi. 63).
The Father affirmed it (Matt. iii. 17).
The Resurrection declared it (Rom. i. 4).
Paul preached it (Acts ix. 20).
Peter confessed it (Matt. xvi. 16).
Demons acknowledged it (Mark iii. 11).
Disciples believed it (Matt. xiv. 33).

21. The Incarnation.

The Word became flesh (John i. 14; 1 Tim. iii. 16).
Partook of flesh and blood (Heb. ii. 14-17, v. 5).
Born of a woman (Gal. iv. 4, with Luke i. 30-35).
Took the form of a servant (Phil. ii. 7; Luke xxii. 27).
In the likeness of sinful flesh (Rom. viii. 3; 1 Pet. iii. 18).
The Holy One of God (Mark i. 24; Acts iii. 14).
The Image of His Person (Heb. i. 2; John i. 18).

22. The Deity of Christ.

Proclaimed by the Father (Matt. i. 23; John i. 1).
Claimed by the Son (John x. 30; John v. 21; Rev. i. 8).
Witnessed by the Spirit (Heb. i. 8; 1 Pet. iii. 15 R.V.).
Owned by Angels (Heb. i. 6; Rev. v. 11-12).
Confessed by Saints (John xx. 28; Rom. ix. 5).
Feared by Demons (Mark v. 7; Jas. ii. 19).
Manifested by His Works (Luke vii. 20; John v. 36).

23. The Resurrection of Christ.

Attributed to the Father (Rom. vi. 4; Col. ii. 12).
Attributed to the Son (John x. 18; Luke xxiv. 6-7).
Attributed to the Spirit (1 Pet. iii. 18; Rom. viii. 11).

24. The Perfect Sacrifice of Christ.

Offered once for all upon the Cross.

It was an Expiation (Rom. viii. 3; Gal. i. 4).
It was a Death Sentence (Gal. iii. 13; 2 Cor. v. 23).
It was for a Propitiation (Rom. iii. 23; 1 John ii. 2).
It was a Purchase (1 Cor. vi. 20; Acts xx. 28).
It was a Peacemaking (Col. i. 20; Isa. liii. 5).

25.   Four Aspects of Resurrection.

The Seal of a Finished Work (Acts xiii. 29-30).
The Sign of a Glorious Triumph (Heb. ii. 14; Eph. iv. 8).
The Pledge of a Coming Resurrection (1 Cor. xv. 20-22).
The Certainty of a Future Judgment (Acts xvii. 31).

26.   The Present Ministry of Christ.

In Heaven for His Saints.

As their Shepherd (Heb. xiii. 20)—Guiding.
As their High Priest (Heb. iv. 14, with ii. 17)—Succoring.
As their Advocate (1 John ii. 2)—Interceding.
As their Lord (Acts ii. 36)—Ruling.

27.   The Coming of the Lord

FOR His Saints.

The Lord's Promise (John xiv. 3; Rev. xxii. 7, 12, 20).
A Personal Return (Acts i. 11; Rev. xxii. 16).
Descends to the Air (1 Thess. iv. 16).
The Dead in Christ Rise (1 Thess. iv. 16; 1 Cor. xv. 52).
The Living Are Changed (1 Thess. iv. 17; 1 Cor. xv. 51).
Caught up Together (1 Thess. iv. 17; 2 Thess. ii. 1).
With, and Like the Lord (1 Thess. iv. 17).

28.   The Appearing of the Lord

WITH His Saints.

In Majesty and Power (2 Thess. i. 7; Rev. xix. 11).
In Manifested Glory (Matt. xxiv. 30; Titus ii. 12).
With All His Saints (Col. iii. 4; Rom. viii. 19).
To Judge His Enemies (Jude 15; Acts xvii. 31).
To Punish Grace Despisers (2 Thess. i. 9; Acts xiii. 41).
To Destroy Antichrist (2 Thess. ii. 8; Rev. xix. 20).
To Deliver Creation (Rom. viii. 21; Isa. xi. 6).

29. The Judgment of the Dead.

The Judgment Throne (Rev. xx. 11; Psa. lxxxix. 14).
The Seated Judge (John v. 27; Psa. ix. 4).
The Resurrected Culprits (John v. 28-29; Rev. xx. 12).
The Opened Books (Rev. xx. 12); Eccl. xii. 14).
The Final Sentence (Rev. xx. 14, xxi. 8).

30. The Punishment of the Wicked.

Foretold by Patriarchs (Deut. xxxii. 22; Job xxxvi. 18).
Warned of by Prophets (Psa. ix. 17; Isa. v. 14, xiv. 9).
Described by the Lord (Matt. xxv. 46; Mark ix. 47).
Taught by Apostles (2 Pet. ii. 9; Heb. x. 29).
Unveiled in Revelation (Rev. xiv. 10, xx. 14-15).
Denied by Scoffers (2 Pet. iii. 4; Jude 18).

31. The Creation of Man.

The Work of God (Gen. i. 26-27, ii. 7).
In His Image (Gen. i. 27, v. 1; Eccl. vii. 29; Jas. iii. 9).
Spirit, Soul, and Body (Gen. ii. 7; 1 Thess. v. 23).
The Unity of Mankind (Acts xvii. 26; Gen. ix. 16).
Man's Eternal Existence (John v. 28-29; Rev. xx. 12).

32. The Fall and Its Consequences.

Adam's Personal Fall (Gen. ii. 17, iii. 7-8).
The Penal Consequences (Rom. v. 12-17; 1 Cor. xv. 22).
The Inherited Nature (Eph. ii. 3; Psa. li. 5).
The Total Depravity (Rom. iii. 9-18, v. 19-20).
The Need of Regeneration (Job xiv. 4; John iii. 3).

33. The Personality of the Spirit.

Described by the Lord Jesus (John xiv. 16-17, xv. 26).
Not an Influence, but a Person (Acts v. 9; Matt. xii. 31-33).
His Words and Works (Acts viii. 29, 39, xiii. 2-4, xvi. 6).
His Attributes and Character (1 Cor. ii. 10; 2 Pet. i. 21).
Sent and Come (John xv. 26; Acts ii. 1-4, v. 32).
Received and Rejected (Acts x. 44; Eph. i. 13; Acts vii. 51).

34. The Designations of the Spirit.

The Comforter, Paraclete, Helper (John xiv. 26).
The Searcher, Revealer, Teacher (1 Cor. ii. 10-14).
The Strengthener, Indweller, Guide (Eph. iii. 16).

35. The Work of the Spirit.

In the World (John xvi. 8-11; 1 Pet. i. 12; 1 Thess. i. 5).
In the Believer (Titus iii. 5; Gal. iv. 6; Rom. viii. 15-26).
In the Church (1 Cor. iii. 16, xii. 4-8; Acts xiii. 2-4).

36. The Opposition to the Spirit.

By the Sinner—Resisted (Acts vii. 51; Heb. x. 29).
In the Saint—Grieved (Eph. iv. 30, with Isa. lxiii. 10).
In the Church—Quenched (1 Thess. v. 19; 1 Cor. xiv. 43).

37. Three Foundation Facts.

Ruin in Sins (Rom. v. 12; 1 Cor. xv. 22; Rom. iii. 23; Psa. li. 5; Eph. ii. 1).
Redemption by Blood (Heb. ix. 22; Types, Gen. iv. 4; Exod. xii. 13; Lev. xvi. 16).
Regeneration by the Spirit (John iii. 5; John vi. 63; Titus iii. 5).

38.　　Seven Fundamental Truths.

The Inspiration of the Scriptures (2 Tim. iii. 16).
The Trinity of the Godhead (Matt. xxviii. 19).
The Divinity of the Lord Jesus (John i. 1).
The Atoning Death of Christ (Heb. ix. 14).
Justification by Faith Alone (Rom. iii. 28).
Salvation, Present and Eternal (Heb. v. 9).
Future Punishment of the Wicked (Matt. xxv. 46).

39.　　The Inspiration of the Scriptures.

Their Divine Origin (2 Tim. iii. 16).
The Human Channels (2 Pet. i. 21; 2 Sam. xxiii. 2).
Their Absolute Purity (Psa. xix. 8; Pro. xxx. 5).
Their Supreme Authority (Psa. cxxxviii. 2; cix. 128).
Accepted by the Lord Jesus (Luke xxiv. 27-45).
Eternal and Imperishable (Matt. xxiv. 35; 1 Pet. i. 25).
Wrested and Corrupted by Men (2 Cor. ii. 17; 2 Pet. iii. 16).
Made Void by Tradition (Mark vii. 13; 2 Tim. iv. 4).

40.　　The Eternal Destiny of Man.

Two Roads and Two Ends (Matt. vi. 13-27).
Two Destinies, Contrasted (1 Pet. iv. 17-18, xxii. 14-15).
Eternal Glory for the Saved (1 Pet. v. 10; 2 Tim. ii. 10).
Eternal Woe for the Lost (Mark ix. 43; 2 Thess. i. 10).

41.　　The Atonement of Christ.

Its Necessity (Heb. ix. 22; Job. xxxiii. 24).
Its Nature (John i. 29; 1 Cor. xv. 3; 1 Pet. iii. 18).
Its Sufficiency (Heb. ix. 12, 25-28, x.; Eph. v. 2).
Its Results (Rom. iii. 25-26; Heb. i. 3, x. 17; Col. i. 20).

42. Atonement in Type and Prophecy.

Types of Christ (Gen. iii. 21, iv. 4, viii. 20; Num. xxi. 9).
Types of His Atoning Death (Gen. vi. 14; Exod. xii. 6, xxx. 16; Lev. xvi. 19).
Foreshadowings (Gen. xxii. 8-10; Exod. xxvii. 1; Lev. i. 3-5).
Prophecies (Isa. liii. 4-12; Dan. ix. 26; Zech. xiii. 7).

43. Atonement in Fact and Testimony.

Made on the Cross (John xix. 30, 34-36; Heb. ix. 14).
Accepted in the Heavens (Heb. ix. 24, x. 12, iv. 14).
Attested by the Resurrection (Acts xiii. 29-30; Rom. iv. 25).
Witnessed to by the Spirit (Heb. x. 15; Acts v. 32).
Proclaimed in the Gospel (1 Cor. xv. 3; Acts x. 43, xiii. 38).
Relied upon by the Believer (Rom. iii. 25, v. 1).

44. Atonement in Result and Celebration.

It Effects Justification (Rom. v. 8).
It Brings to God (Eph. ii. 13).
It Sanctifies (Heb. x. 10, xiii. 12).
It Cleanses (Rev. i. 5; 1 John i. 7).
It Reconciles (Rom. v. 10; 2 Cor. v. 20-21).
Symbolized in Baptism (Rom. vi. 4; Col. ii. 12).
Commemorated in the Lord's Supper (1 Cor. xi. 23-26).

45. The World: Its Course and End.

The Empire of Satan (John xii. 31, xvi. 11; 1 John v. 4).
It Has Rejected Christ (John i. 10, vii. 7).
Christ Came To Save (John iii. 16-17, xii. 47; 1 Tim. i. 15).
All Guilty Before God (Rom. iii. 19).
Its Judgment (John xii. 31; Acts xvii. 31).
Its Doom (1 John i. 17; 2 Pet. iii. 6-8).

46. The Christian's Relation to the World.

Born into the World (John xvi. 21).
Given out of the World (John xvii. 6).
Delivered from the World (Gal. i. 4).
Crucified to the World (Gal. vi. 14).
Not of the World (John xvii. 16).
A Stranger in the World (1 John iii. 2).
Hated by the World (John xvii. 14).

47. The Christian's Place in the World.

Sent into the World (John xvii. 18, xx. 21).
Preaching to the World (Mark xv. 15).
The Light of the World (Phil. ii. 15; Matt. v. 14).
Live Godly in the World (Tit. ii. 12).
Not Conformed to the World (Rom. xii. 2; John xvii. 15).
Love Not the World (1 John ii. 16; 2 Tim. iv. 10).
Passing Through the World (1 Pet. ii. 11).
No Friendship with the World (James iv. 4, i. 27).

48. Divine Love in Varied Aspects.

Love of Compassion (John iii. 16)—For Sinners.
Love of Relationship (1 John iii. 1)—To Children.
Love of Communion (John xiv. 23)—To Obedient Ones.

49. Children of God—Their Position.

A Title of Relationship and Endearment.

Begotten of God (John i. 12; 1 John v. 1-2).
In a New Relationship (Rom. viii. 15; John viii. 35).
Linked with Christ (John xx. 17; Heb. ii. 11).
Heirs and Joint Heirs (Gal. iv. 7; Rom. viii. 17).
Dear Children—Title of Endearment (1 John ii. 12-28).
Unknown by the World (1 John iii. 2; John xv. 18-21).
Waiting for the Manifestation (Rom. viii. 19; Col. iii. 4).

50.   Children of God—Their Progress.

Newborn Babes—Healthy and Growing (1 Pet. ii. 1).
Little Children (1 John ii. 13-18, iii. 18).
Infants, an Unhealthy Condition (Gal. iv. 1; 1 Cor. iii. 1).
Young Men (1 John ii. 14-17; Prov. xx. 29).
Fathers, Full Grown (1 John ii. 13-14; 1 Cor. iv. 15).

51.   Children of God—Their Prospects.

They shall see the Lord (1 John iii. 2; 1 Cor. xiii. 12).
They shall be like Him (1 John iii. 2; 2 Thess. i. 10).
They will dwell in the Father's House (John xiv. 2-3).
They will be manifested in glory (Rom. viii. 19-21).
They will be forever with the Lord (Rev. xxii. 7).

52.   Sons of God.

A Title of Dignity and Manifestation of Character.

We Become Sons by Faith (Gal. iii. 24; John i. 12).
Possess the Spirit of Sons (Gal. iv. 6; Rom. viii. 14).
To Enjoy the Place of Sons (Luke xv. 24; Rom. viii. 14).
To Manifest the Character of Sons (Matt. v. 45-48).
Receive the Training of Sons (Heb. xii. 5-11; 1 Pet. i. 17).
To Be Conformed to Christ (Rom. viii. 30; 1 John iii. 2).

53.   The Lordship of Christ.

Exalted as Lord (Acts ii. 36; Phil. ii. 9-10).
All Authority Given Him (Matt. xxviii. 18; John xvii. 2).
Confessed Lord in Conversion (Rom. x. 9 R.V.).
Sanctified Lord in the Heart (1 Pet. iii. 15 R.V.)
Owned as Lord in the Life (Col. iii. 17).
Acknowledged Lord in the Church (1 Cor. xiv. 37).
To Be Honored as Lord by All (Phil. ii. 10).

BIBLE READINGS

54.   **Seven "Kingdoms"**

In the New Testament.

Kingdom of God (John iii. 3).
Kingdom of Heaven (Matt. iii. 2).
Kingdom of His Dear Son (Col. i. 13).
Kingdom of the Father (Matt. xiii. 23).
Kingdom of the Son of Man (Luke i. 33).
Kingdom Everlasting (2 Pet. i. 11).

55.   **Seven "Better Things"**

In the Epistle to the Hebrews.

Better Testament (Chap. vii. 22).
Better Sacrifice (Chap. ix. 23).
Better Promises (Chap. viii. 6).
Better Hope (Chap. vii. 19).
Better Substance (Chap. x. 34).
Better Country (Chap. xi. 16).
Better Resurrection (Chap. xi. 35).

56.   **Similes of Spiritual Growth.**

As a Seed (Mark iv. 27)—In Steadiness.
As a Lily (Hos. xiv. 5)—In Lowliness.
As a Cedar (Psa. cii. 12)—In Strength.
As a Psalm (Psa. xcii. 12)—In Uprightness.
As a Vine (Hos. xiv. 7)—In Fruitfulness.

57.   Threefold Work of the Spirit.

The Spirit Regenerating (John iii. 5).
The Spirit Indwelling (John iv. 14).
The Spirit Outflowing (John vii. 38).

58.   Christian Readiness.

Ready To Answer (1 Pet. iii. 15).
Ready To Preach (Rom. i. 15).
Ready To Distribute (1 Tim. iv. 18).
Ready for Every Good Work (Titus iii. 1).
Ready To Die (Acts xxi. 13).
Ready To Meet the Lord (Luke xii. 36).
Ready To Enter the Glory (Matt. xxv. 10).

59.   "Daily" Things in Christian Life.

Which maintain the Soul in a good condition.

Daily Renewing of inner man (2 Cor. iv. 16).
Daily Reading of the Word (Neh. viii. 18).
Daily Prayer to the Lord (Psa. lxxvi. 3).
Daily Praising of the Lord (Psa. lxxii. 15).
Daily Exhortation of one another (Heb. iii. 13).
Daily Cross to bear (Luke ix. 23).

60.   Rest in Seven Aspects.

Creation Rest (Gen. ii. 2)—Broken by Sin.
Redemption Rest (Zeph. iii. 17)—Secured in Christ.
The Sinner's Rest (Matt. xi. 28)—By Coming to Christ.
The Saint's Rest (Matt. xi. 29)—In Learning of Christ.
The Servant's Rest (Mark vi. 30)—In Communion with Christ.
Paradise Rest (Rev. xvi. 13, with 2 Cor. v. 8-9)—Present.
Eternal Rest (Heb. iv. 9; Rev. xxii. 5)—Future.

61. **New Creation.**

A New Birth (John iii. 3)—Its Entrance.
A New Man (Col. iii. 10)—Its Characteristic.
A New Life (Rom. vi. 4)—Its Manifestation.
A New Song (Psa. xl. 3)—Its Melody.
A New Path (Heb. x. 20)—Its Highway.
A New City (Rev. xxi. 2)—Its Consummation.

62. **The Life of Faith.**

Obedience of Faith (Rom. xvi. 26)—Brings Salvation.
Living by Faith (Gal. ii. 20)—For Sustenance.
Walking by Faith (2 Cor. v. 7)—In Obedience.
Praying in Faith (Jas. v. 15)—Brings Blessing.
Fighting in Faith (1 Tim. vi. 12)—Gives Victory.

63. **Four Things Belonging to Christ.**

As seen in the Epistle to the Philippians.

The Gospel of Christ (Chap. i. 27)—Our Theme.
The Work of Christ (Chap. iii. 30)—Our Employment.
The Knowledge of Christ (Chap. iii. 8)—Our Study.
The Power of Christ (Chap. iv. 13)—Our Strength.

64. **The Holy Spirit**

In the Believer—Experimentally.

Bears Witness (Rom. viii. 16)—To Sonship.
Sheds Love Abroad (Rom. v. 5)—In Experience.
Strengthens (Eph. iii. 16)—For Service.
Intercedes (Rom. viii. 11)—In Prayer.
Leads (Rom. viii. 14)—In Obedience.
Produces Fruit (Gal. v. 22)—In Life.
Gives Utterance (Acts ii. 4)—In Testimony.

65.   **The Holy Spirit**

In the Believer—Officially.

In His Heart (Gal. iv. 6)—As a Son.
On His Person (Eph. i. 13)—As a Seal.
In His Body (1 Cor. vi. 19)—As a Temple.
    The *First* establishes communion WITH God.
    The *Second* secures him FOR God.
    The *Third* sets him apart TO God.

66.   **"In the Spirit."**

Live in the Spirit (Gal. v. 25)—Christian Life.
Walk in the Spirit (Gal. v. 25)—Christian Walk.
Pray in the Spirit (Eph. vi. 18)—Christian Devotion.
Worship in the Spirit (Phil. iii. 3)—Christian Priesthood.
Love in the Spirit (Col. i. 8)—Christian Brotherhood.

67.   **Christ's Calls to His Own.**

Arise from Among the Dead (Eph. v. 14)—Separation.
Arise, Let Us Go Hence (John xiv. 31)—Communion.
Arise and Walk (Matt. ix. 5)—Discipleship.
Arise and Come Away (Song of Sol. ii. 13)—Glory.

68.   **The Lord's People**

Are described in the Word as

A Chosen People (Deut. vii. 6; 1 Pet. 2:9).
A Redeemed People (Exod. xv. 13; Eph. i. 7).
A Peculiar People (Deut. xiv. 2; Titus ii. 14).
A Separated People (Exod. xxxiii. 16; John xv. 19).
A Holy People (Deut. vii. 6; 1 Pet. i. 15).
A Happy People (Deut. xxxiii. 29; John xv. 11).

69.   **Four "Withouts"**

In the Epistle to the Hebrews.

"Without Shedding of Blood" (Heb. ix. 22)—No Remission.
"Without Faith" (Heb. xi. 6)—No Pleasing God.
"Without Holiness" (Heb. xii. 14)—No Heaven.
"Without Chastisement" (Heb. xii. 8)—No Sonship.

70.   "Precious" Things in Peter's Epistles.

Precious Blood (1 Pet. i. 19)—To Redeem.
Precious Faith (1 Pet. i. 7)—To Try.
Precious Stone (1 Pet. ii. 4)—To Uphold.
Precious Christ (1 Pet. ii. 7)—To Love.
Precious Promises (2 Pet. i. 4)—To Plead.

71.   Crowns.

Rewards for Faithful Service here.

Crown of Life (Rev. ii. 16)—The Martyr's Reward.
Crown of Righteousness (2 Tim. iv. 8)—The Steward's Reward.
Crown of Glory (1 Pet. v. 4)—The Shepherd's Reward.

72.   Divine Love in Seven Aspects.

Love Manifested (1 John iv. 9)—In the Gift of Christ.
Love Commended (Rom. v. 8)—At the Cross.
Love Bestowed (1 John iii. 1)—In Our Sonship.
Love Believed (1 John iv. 16)—By the Sinner.
Love Perceived (1 John iii. 16)—By the Saint.
Love Shed Abroad (Rom. v. 5)—In the Spirit.
Love Dwelling (1 John iii. 17)—In the Heart.

73. The Christian Stewardship.

The Master's Appointment (Matt. xxv. 14; Mark xiii. 34).
The Steward's Responsibility (1 Cor. iv. 1-3; 2 Tim. ii. 2).
The Trust Committed (1 Thess. ii. 4; 2 Tim. i. 14).
  The Gospel for all (Mark xv. 15; Rom. i. 4).
  The Truth, all of it (Matt. xxviii. 20; Acts xx. 27).
The Steward's Character (Tit. ii. 7; 1 Cor. iv. 2).
  A Good Steward (1 Pet. iv. 10)—Dispensing.
  A Wise Steward (Luke xii. 42)—Discriminating.
  An Unjust Steward (Luke xvi. 1)—Wasting.
The Reckoning Day (2 Cor. v. 9; 1 Cor. iv. 5).

74. Faith.

The Word of Faith (Rom. x. 8)—The Preacher's Message.
The Hearing of Faith (Gal. iii. 2)—The Hearer's Responsibility.
The Obedience of Faith (Rom. xvi. 16)—The Receiver's Response.
The Righteousness of Faith (Rom. iv. 13)—The Believer's Position.
The Walk of Faith (2 Cor. v. 6)—The Believer's Path
The Work of Faith (1 Thess. i. 3)—The Christian's Service.
The Fight of Faith (1 Tim. vi. 12)—The Soldier's Warfare.

75. Sevenfold View of the Spirit.

The Spirit of Life (Rom. viii. 2).
The Spirit of Sonship (Rom. viii. 15).
The Spirit of Promise (Eph. i. 13).
The Spirit of Power (2 Tim. i. 7).
The Spirit of Truth (John xiv. 17).
The Spirit of Wisdom (Eph. i. 14).
The Spirit of Glory (1 Pet. iv. 14).

76. Separation

From the World (John xv. 19; Gal. i. 4; vi. 14).
From the Darkness (1 Pet. ii. 9; Eph. v. 8; 2 Cor. vi. 14).
From False Professors (2 Tim. iii. 1-5; 2 Cor. vi. 17).
From Teachers of Error (1 Tim. 1. 4; iv. 7; vi. 5).

77. Amalgamations

Which Are Forbidden in God's Word.

Of Law and Grace (Acts xv. 1-24; Gal. iii. 2; v. 4).
Of Truth and Tradition (Mark vi. 8-13; 2 Tim. iv. 3).
Of Saints and Sinners (2 Cor. vi. 14; 2 Tim. ii. 21).

78. Seven "New Things"

Which All Believers Now Possess.

REPENTANCE—A new MIND about God (Acts xx. 21).
JUSTIFICATION—A new STATE before God (Rom. iv. 25).
REGENERATION—A new LIFE from God (Titus iii. 5).
CONVERSION—A new ATTITUDE toward God (Matt. xviii. 3).
SONSHIP—A new RELATIONSHIP with God (1 John iii. 1).
SANCTIFICATION—A new POSITION before God (Jude i.)
GLORIFICATION—A new PLACE with God (Rom. viii. 30).

79. Our God

Is Revealed in the Word as

The God of all Grace (1 Pet. v. 10).
The God of Peace (Heb. xiii. 20).
The God of all Comfort (2 Cor. i. 3).
The God of Patience (Rom. xv. 5).
The God of Hope (Rom. xv. 13).
The God of Glory (Acts vii. 2).
"This God is OUR God for ever" (Psa. xlviii. 14).

80. Living.

The Living God (1 Tim. iv. 10)—Our Trust.
The Living Christ (1 Pet. ii. 4)—Our Foundation.
The Living Spirit (John iv. 11)—Our Refreshment.
The Living Way (Heb. x. 20)—Our Access.
The Living Hope (1 Pet. i. 3)—Our Expectation.

81.   In the Name.

Salvation in the Name (Acts iv. 12).
Remission in the Name (Acts x. 43).
Baptized in the Name (Acts xix. 5).
Gathered unto the Name (Matt. xviii. 20).
Going Forth in the Name (3 John 7).
Suffering for the Name (1 Pet. iv. 16).
Not Denying the Name (Rev. iii. 8).

82.   Progress in Grace.

Saved by Grace (Eph. ii. 9).
Standing in Grace (Rom. v. 2).
Taught by Grace (Titus ii. 12).
Growing in Grace (2 Pet. iii. 18).
Speaking in Grace (Col. iv. 6).
Ministering in Grace (1 Pet. iv. 10).

83.   Partakers.

Of His Promise in Christ (Eph. iii. 6)—Salvation.
Of the Divine Nature (2 Pet. ii. 4)—Regeneration.
Of the Inheritance (Col. i. 12)—Competency.
Of the Heavenly Calling (Heb. iii. 1)—Position.
Of Christ's Sufferings (1 Pet. iv. 13)—Discipleship.
Of Fatherly Chastisement (Heb. xii. 6)—Discipline.
Of the Glory (1 Pet. v. 1)—Prospect.

84.   Seven Jehovah Titles

Jehovah-Jireh—The Lord will Provide (Gen. xxii. 14).
Jehovah-Tsidkenu—The Lord our Righteousness (Jer. xxiii. 6).
Jehovah-Ropheka—The Lord our Healer (Exod. xv. 26).
Jehovah-Shalom—The Lord our Peace (Judges vi. 24).

Jehovah-Rophi—The Lord our Shepherd (Psa. xxiii. 1).
Jehovah-Nissi—The Lord our Banner (Exod. xvii. 15).
Jehovah Shammah—The Lord is there (Ezek. xlviii. 35).

These seven Titles embrace all the fullness of Jehovah's Name manifested in Christ for His people, completely meeting all their need from guilt to glory.

85. Godliness

The Form of Godliness (2 Tim. iii. 5)—The Hypocrite.
The Mystery of Godliness (1 Tim. iii. 16)—The Saviour.
The Doctrine of Godliness (1 Tim. vi. 3)—The Truth.
The Profession of Godliness (1 Tim. ii. 15)—The Believer's Confession.
The Practice of Godliness (1 Tim. iv .7)—The Believer's Walk.
The Pursuit of Godliness (1 Tim. vi. 11)—The Believer's Object.

86. The Believer's Heart.

A Broken Heart (Psa. li. 17)—Confesses Sin.
An Opened Heart (Acts xvi. 14)—Receives the Word.
A Single Heart (Eph. vi. 5)—Serves Faithfully.
A Pure Heart (1 Pet. i. 22)—Loves Fervently.
A True Heart (Heb. x. 22)—Draws Near to God.
A Purposed Heart (Acts xi. 23)—Cleaves to the Lord.
An Evil Heart (Heb. iii. 12)—Departs from God.

87. Divine Unity.

Children in one Family—One Father (John xx. 17).
Disciples in one School—One Teacher (John xiii. 13-35).
Sheep in one Flock—One Shepherd (John x. 16 R.V.).
Members of one Body—One Head (Eph. iv. 15).
Stones in one Building—One Foundation (1 Cor. iii. 11).

88. Salvation Sevenfold.

Saved by Grace (Eph. ii. 5)—Actually.
Saved through Faith (Eph. ii. 8)—Instrumentally.
Saved by Works (James ii. 14)—Evidentially.
Saved through Water (1 Pet. iii. 21)—Confessedly.
Saved by His Life (Rom. v. 9)—Practically.
Saved in Hope (Rom. viii. 24)—Prospectively.
Saved at His Coming (Phil. iii. 20)—Eternally.

89. Sevenfold Virtue of Christ's Blood.

It procures Redemption (Eph. i. 6).
It secures Justification (Rom. v. 9).
It ensures Cleansing (1 John 1. 7).
It makes Peace (Col. i. 20).
It effects Sanctification (Heb. xiii. 12).
It gives Nearness (Eph. ii. 13).
It brings Victory (Rev. xii. 11).

90. The Word of God.

Its Divine Inspiration (2 Tim. iii. 16).
Its Absolute Purity (Psa. xii. 6).
Its Supreme Authority (Psa. cxix. 128).
Its Perfect Unity (John x. 35).
Its Eternal Permanency (1 Pet. i. 25).
 Other Texts on each branch of the subject abound.

91. Divine Discipline.

Its Subjects, Believers (Heb. xii. 5-7; 2 Sam. vii. 14; Amos iii. 3).
Its Nature, parental, not judicial (1 Pet. i. 14-17; 1 Cor. xi. 32).
Its Instruments, The Word (Titus ii. 12); The Knife (John xv. 4, &c).
Its Objects, Profit, Fruit, Holiness (Heb. xii. 10-11).

92.   **Divine Riches.**

Riches of Mercy (Eph. ii. 4).
Riches of Grace (Eph. i. 7).
Riches of Goodness (Rom. ii. 4).
Riches of Glory (Phil. iv. 19).

93.   **The Lamb of God.**

The Lamb Provided (Gen. xxii. 8; Job xxxiii. 24).
The Lamb Described (Exod. xii. 5-6; 1 Pet. i. 19).
The Lamb Revealed (John i. 29-36; Matt. xi. 29).
The Lamb Slain (Exod. xii. 6-7; Isa. liii. 7).
The Lamb Glorified (Rev. v. 6-12, vii. 17).
The Lamb Reigning (Rev. xxii. 1-3).

94.   **Divine Revelations.**

The word "Revelation" means Unveiling.

God's righteousness revealed (Rom. i. 17)—In the Gospel.
Christ revealed (Gal. i. 16)—To the Soul.
The Mystery revealed (Eph. ii. 3)—Union with Christ.
The Glory to be revealed (Rom. viii. 18)—At His Coming.
The Man of Sin revealed (2 Thess. ii. 8)—To Christ Rejecters.

95.   **Eternal Blessings.**

Purchased with an Eternal Redemption (Heb. ix. 12).
Saved with an Eternal Salvation (Heb. v. 9).
Possessed of an Eternal Life (John iii. 15).
Called to an Eternal Glory (1 Pet. v. 10).
Waiting for an Eternal Home (2 Cor. v. 1).

96.   "At Jesus' Feet."

For Forgiveness (Luke vii. 38).
For Healing (Matt. xv. 3).
For Teaching (Luke x. 39).
In Distress (John xi. 32).
In Prayer (Luke viii. 41).
In Fear (Rev. i. 17).
In Worship (Luke xvii. 16).

97.   Christ Our Keeper.

Kept by His Power (1 Pet. 1. 5).
Kept from Falling (Jude 24).
Kept from All Evil (2 Thess. iii. 3).
Kept in Peace (Isa. xxvi. 3).
Kept as the Apple of His Eye (Deut. xxxii. 10).
Kept from the Temptation (Rev. iii. 10).
Kept for Eternal Glory (John xvii. 12).

98.   Suffering for Christ

Suffering for Righteousness' Sake (1 Pet. iii. 14).
Suffering for Godly Living (2 Tim. ii. 12).
Suffering for the Kingdom of God (2 Thess. i. 5).
Suffering as a Christian (1 Pet. iv. 16).
Suffering for Christ's Sake (Phil. i. 29).
Suffering and Glory (1 Pet. v. 1).

99.   Jesus Christ Our Lord

Exalted as Lord (Acts ii. 36).
Confessed as Lord (Rom. x. 9).
Owned as Lord (Acts ix. 6).
Praised as Lord (Psa. ix. 11).
Obeyed as Lord (Col. iii. 17).
Served as Lord (Col. iii. 24).
Denied as Lord (Jude 14).

100. The Christian Pilgrim.

1 Peter ii. 11, with Heb. xi. 13.

His Path (Heb. xiii. 13).
His Support (Phil. iv. 13).
His Foes (1 Pet. ii. 11).
His Temptations (Jas. i. 2).
His City Home (Heb. xi. 10).
His Friends (Heb. xi. 13).
His Inheritance (1 Pet. i. 4).

101. New Testament Mysteries.

The Mystery of Godliness (1 Tim. iii. 16)—Christ Personally.
The Mystery Kept Secret (Rom. xvi. 25)—The Truth Revealed.
The Mystery of the Faith (1 Tim. iii. 9)—The Truth Held Fast.
The Mystery of Christ (Eph. v. 31-32)—Christ and the Church.
The Mystery of Union (Eph. iii. 3)—Jew and Gentile One.
The Mystery of Lawlessness (2 Thess. ii. 7 R.V.)—Satan's Coun-
    terfeits.
The Mystery of Glorification (1 Cor. xv. 31)—At Christ's Coming.

102. The People of God

Are

A Saved People (Deut. xxxiii. 29).
A Separated People (Lev. xx. 24).
A Happy People (Psa. cxliv. 15).
A Holy People (Deut. vii. 6).
A Peculiar People (1 Pet. ii. 9).

103. What the Gospel Brings

To All Who Believe It.

Saved by the Gospel (Rom. i. 16).
Begotten through the Gospel (1 Cor. iv. 15).
Peace received in the Gospel (Rom. x. 15).
Blessing through the Gospel (Rom. xv. 29).
Glory revealed by the Gospel (1 Tim. i. 11 R.V.).

104.   Things that Accompany Salvation.

(Hebrews vi. 9).

The *Knowledge* of Salvation (Luke i. 77).
The *Joy* of Salvation (Psa. li. 12).
The *Strength* of Salvation (Isa. xxxiii. 6).
The *Wells* of Salvation (Isa. xii. 3).
The *Cup* of Salvation (Psa. cxvi. 13).
The *Hope* of Salvation (Eph. vi. 17).

105.   "With Christ."

Dead with Christ (Rom. vi. 4).
Buried with Christ (Col. ii. 12).
Quickened with Christ (Col. ii. 12).
Risen with Christ (Col. iii. 1).
Glorified with Christ (Rom. viii. 17).

106.   The Christian Path.

Walk in Light (1 John i. 7).
Walk in Love (Eph. v. 2).
Walk in the Spirit (Gal. v. 16).
Walk in Truth (3 John 4).
Walk in Good Works (Eph. ii. 10).
Walk in Wisdom (Col. iv. 5).
Walk Circumspectly (Eph. v. 15).

107.   A Seven-Linked Chain of Fellowship.

Fellow-heirs (Eph. iii. 6)—Of One Inheritance.
Fellow-members (Eph. iii. 6 R.V.)—Of One Body.
Fellow-partakers (Eph. iii. 6 R.V.)—Of One Calling.
Fellow-citizens (Eph. ii. 19)—Of One Home.
Fellow-laborers (Phil. iv. 3)—Of One Master.
Fellow-soldiers (Phil. ii. 25)—In One Warfare.
Fellow-prisoners (Rom. xvi. 7)—With One Hope.

108.   The Unequal Yoke

Between Saved and Unsaved Forbidden.

In Matrimony (1 Cor. vii. 39, with Deut. vii. 3).
In Commerce (Deut. xxii. 10; Amos iii. 2).
In Religion (2 Cor. vi. 14; 2 Tim. iii. 5).
In Social Circle (Eph. v. 7-11; Rom. xii. 2).
The *First* was ignored by Israel (Jud. ii. 6; Neh. xiii. 23).
The *Second* set aside by Dinah (Gen. xxxiv. 1).
The *Third* disobeyed by Jehoshaphat (2 Chron. xx. 35).
The *Fourth* transgressed by the Young Prophet (1 Kings xiii.
    17-22).

109.   God's Truth in Divine Order.

Key Words of the First Seven Books.

In GENESIS is the *Election* and *Call* of God's People.
In EXODUS, their *Redemption* and *Separation*.
In LEVITICUS, their *Acceptance* and *Worship*.
In NUMBERS, their *Walk* and *Warfare*.
In DEUTERONOMY, their *Government* and *Testimony*.
In JOSHUA, their *Warfare* and *Inheritance*.
In JUDGES, their *Declension* and *Defeat*.

110.   Divine Fullness.

Fullness of Grace (John i. 16)—Our Resource.
Fullness of Blessing (Rom. xv. 29)—Our Privilege.
Fullness of Joy (John xv. 11)—Our Portion.
Fullness of Power (Acts vi. 8)—Our Strength.
Fullness of God (Eph. iii. 19)—Our Consummation.

111.   Sins Against the Holy Spirit.

He is Resisted (Acts vii. 51)—By the World.
He is Grieved (Eph. iv. 30)—By the Believer.
He is Quenched (1 Thess. v. 19)—In the Church.
The *First* is by Rejection of the Gospel.
The *Second* through trifling with Sin.
The *Third* by man's arrangements hindering His work.

112. Holiness.

Its Pattern in Christ (Acts iv. 27).
Its Standard in the World (2 Pet. ii. 21; Col. i. 22).
How Produced (Eph. i. 4, iv. 24, v. 27).
How Maintained (1 Tim. iv. 12; 2 Tim. ii. 21).
Personal (1 Pet. i. 15; 2 Pet. iii. 11).
Social (2 Cor. vii. 1; 1 Thess. iv. 7).
Ecclesiastical (Psa. xciii. 5; 1 Cor. iii. 11).

113. Vital Godliness.

The Word means Piety, Reverence.

Its Lack in the World (Psa. xii. 1).
Its Empty Form in Christendom (2 Tim. iii. 5).
Its Pattern and Source in Christ (1 Tim. iii. 16; Heb. v. 7).
Its Power for Believers (2 Pet. i. 3; 2 Tim. iii. 16).
Its Pursuit by Believers (1 Tim. iv. 7, vi. 11).
Its Treatment from the World (2 Tim. iii. 12).
Its Importance in View of Eternity (2 Pet. iii. 16).

114. Secret of a Peaceful Life.

Peace with God (Rom. v. 1)—By Faith.
Peace Multiplied (2 Pet. i. 2)—Through Knowledge.
Peace of God (Phil. iv. 6-7)—By Prayerfulness.
Peace Ruling (Col. iii. 15)—In Submission.
God of Peace (Phil. iv. 9)—By Obedience.
Great Peace (Psa. cxix. 165)—By Loving the Word.
Perfect Peace (Isa. xxvi. 3)—Through Trusting.

115. Temptation,

Trials, tests, sent or allowed by God.

Divers Temptations (Jas. i. 2)—Of various kinds.
Manifold Temptations (1 Pet. i. 6)—From various sources.
Their Origin, Flesh (Jas. i. 14); Devil (1 Thess. iii. 5).
Their Uses, Test (1 Pet. i. 7); Strengthen (1 Pet. v. 10).
The Way of Victory (Jas. i. 12, R.V.)—Endurance.
The Power of Deliverance (1 Cor. x. 12; 2 Pet. ii. 8-9).
The Result and Reward (Jas. i. 2-12).

BIBLE SUBJECTS

116.   **Four Titles of Believers.**

In John xv.

Disciples (Verse 8)—Learning of Christ.
Friends (Verse 15)—Communing with Christ.
Servants (Verse 20)—Working for Christ.
Witnesses (Verse 27)—Testifying to Christ.

117.   **Three Circles for Prayer.**

"All Saints" (Eph. vi. 18, with Col. i. 3; iv. 12).
"All Men" (1 Tim. ii. 1, with Matt. v. 14).
"All Things" (Matt. xxi. 12, with Phil. iv. 6).

118.   **A Threefold Manner of Life.**

"Soberly"—in regard to ourselves (Rom. xii. 3).
"Righteously"—in respect of the world (Prov. ii. 20).
"Godly"—in relation to God (2 Tim. iii. 12).

119.   **The Calling of the Believers.**

Called out of Darkness (1 Pet. ii. 9).
Called Saints (Rom. i. 7 R.V.).
Called Sons of God (1 John iii. 1).
Called by Grace (Gal. i. 15).
Called to Glory (1 Pet. v. 9).
Called unto Fellowship (1 Cor. i. 9).
Called into Liberty (Gal. v. 13).
"Walk worthy of the calling" (Eph. iv. 1 R.V.).

120.   Four Aspects of Christian Life.

Sons to love (1 John v. 2; Col. i. 4).
Servants to obey (2 Tim. ii. 24; Rom. vi. 22).
Soldiers to fight (2 Tim. ii. 3; 1 Tim. vi. 12).
Stewards to occupy (Titus i. 7; Luke xix. 13).

121. Three Attitudes of the Servant of the Lord.

Sitting before the Lord (2 Sam. vii. 18)—In Rest.
Standing before the Lord (1 Kings xvii. 1)—In Readiness.
Speaking before the Lord (2 Cor. xii. 19)—In Testimony.

122.   The Christian's Conversation.

His *former* Conversation (Eph. iv. 22)
Was "Vain" (1 Pet. i. 18),
Or "Filthy" (2 Pet. ii. 7).
It is now
"Holy" before God (1 Pet. iii. 11).
"Chaste" in the Home (1 Pet. iii. 1).
"Honest" in the Business (1 Pet. ii. 12).
"Good" in the World (1 Pet. iii. 16).

123.   Symbols of God's Care.

Of His People.

As a *Mother* comforteth (Isa. lxvi. 13).
As a *Father* pitieth (Psa. ciii. 13).
As a *Nurse* cherisheth (1 Thess. ii. 7).
As a *Shepherd* seeketh (Ezek. xxxiv. 12).
As a *Hen* gathereth (Matt. xxiii. 37).
As an *Eagle* fluttereth (Deut. xxxii. 11).
As a *Bridegroom* rejoiceth (Isa. lxii. 5).

124.　　A Sevenfold Use of the Word.

Born Again by the Word (1 Pet. i. 23; James i. 18).
Cleansed by the Word (Eph. v. 26; Psa. cxix. 9).
Saved by the Word (1 Tim. iv. 16; Jas. i. 21).
Growing by the Word (1 Pet. ii. 2; Jer. xv. 16).
Sanctified by the Word (John xvii. 17; 1 Tim. iv. 5).
Enlightened by the Word (Psa. xix. 8; cxix. 105).
Kept by the Word (Psa. xvii. 4; Rev. iii. 10).

125.　The Believer's Heavenly Possessions.

A *Saviour* in Heaven (Acts v. 31; Phil. iii. 20).
A *Master* in Heaven (Eph. vi. 9; Acts ix. 6).
His *Name* written in Heaven (Luke x. 20; Phil. iv. 3).
His *Citizenship* in Heaven (Phil. iii. 20; Heb. xii. 22).
His *Hope* in Heaven (Col. i. 5; 1 John iii. 3).
His *Inheritance* in Heaven (1 Pet. i. 4; Eph. i. 3).
His *Reward* in Heaven (Luke vi. 23; Rev. xxii. 12).

126.　　God's Infinite Things.

RICHES that are unsearchable (Eph. iii. 8).
JOY that is unspeakable (1 Pet. i. 8).
PEACE that passeth understanding (Phil. iv. 7).
LOVE that passeth knowledge (Eph. iii. 19).
WAYS past finding out (Rom. xi. 33).

127.　　Things in Which To "Abound."

Abound in Faith (2 Cor. viii. 7).
Abound in Hope (Rom. xv. 13).
Abound in Love (Phil. i. 9).
Abound in Good Works (2 Cor. ix. 8).

128.   Things "Laid Up" for Believers.

The Lord's Goodness (Psa. xxxi. 19).
The Hope of Glory (Col. i. 5).
The Crown of Righteousness (2 Tim. iv. 6).

129.   "Consider Him."

In Humiliation (Heb. xii. 3)—Our Example.
In Exaltation (Heb. iii. 1)—Our Representative.

130.   The Powers of Satan.

Satan's Seat (Rev. ii. 13)—His Political Power (John xii. 31).
Satan's Depths (Rev. ii. 24)—His Deceptive Wiles (Rev. xx. 3-10).
Satan's Synagogue (Rev. iii. 9)—His Religious Devices (2 Cor.
     iv. 4).
In the *First* he appears as "a Roaring Lion" (1 Pet. v. 9).
In the *Second* as a Subtle Serpent (2 Cor. x. 3).
In the *Third* as an Angel of LIght (2 Cor. x. 14).

131.   "Unto Him."

"Unto him shall the gathering of the people be" (Gen. xlix. 10).

For Salvation (Luke xv. 1).
For Teaching (Mark vi. 30).
For Worship (Heb. xiii. 13).
For Fellowship (Matt. xviii. 20).
In Glory (2 Thess. ii. 1).

132.   Abundant Grace.

Grace to Save (Eph. ii. 9).
Grace to Establish (Heb. xiii. 9).
Grace to Sustain (2 Cor. ix. 8).
Grace to Serve (1 Cor. xv. 10).

133. The Name of Jesus.

The Source of *Salvation* (Acts iv. 12).
The Authority in *Baptism* (Acts x. 48).
The Center of *Gathering* (Matt. xviii. 20).
The Power in *Discipline* (1 Cor. v. 4).
The Motive in *Service* (3 John 7).
The Plea in *Prayer* (John xiv. 14).
The Rule in *Everything* (Col. iii. 17).

134. "All Saints."

In the Ephesian Epistle.

"Love *to* all Saints" (Chap. 1. 15).
"Comprehend *with* all Saints" (Chap. iii. 18).
"Prayer *for* all Saints" (Chap. vi. 18).

135. Fellowship in Four Aspects.

Fellowship of Life (1 John i. 1-3).
Fellowship in Light (1 John i. 7).
Fellowship of the Church (1 Cor. i. 10; Acts ii. 42).
Fellowship in Service (1 Cor. iii. 9 R.V.; Col. iv. 10).

136. Christ in Hebrews.

The Simpurger (Chap. i. 3)—To Clear.
The Victory (Chap. ii. 15)—To Deliver.
The Apostle (Chap. iii. 1)—To Speak.
The High Priest (Chap. iv. 14)—To Succor.
The Forerunner (Chap. vii. 20)—To Represent.
The Coming One (Chap. x. 37)—To Welcome.

137. Threefold Rejoicing.

In God's Salvation (Psa. lx. 14, with I Pet. 1. 6).
In Christ Jesus (Phil. iii. 3, with 1 Pet. i. 8).
In the Lord (Phil. iv. 10, with Hab. iii. 18).

138.   A Double Testimony for Christ

By a Young Convert.

Go home and *tell* (Mark v. 19)—The Lips.
Return and *show* (Luke viii. 39)—The Life.

139.   A Good Minister.

As seen in Apollos (Acts xviii. 24-25).
"An Eloquent Man."
"Mighty in the Scriptures."
"Instructed in the Way of the Lord."
"Fervent in Spirit."

These four when combined, make "a good minister of Jesus Christ" (1 Tim. iv. 6).

140.   "Till He Come."

Show the Lord's Death (1 Cor. xi. 26)—Worshippers.
Hold Fast His Truth (Rev. ii. 25)—Warriors.
Occupy in His Service (Luke xix. 13)—Workers.

141.   Our Calling.

Called Sons of God (1 John iii. 1)—By the Father.
Called Christians (Acts xi. 26)—By the Son.
Called Saints (Rom. i. 7)—By the Spirit.

142.   Three Great Gospel Blessings.

Procured at the Cross, Proclaimed in the Gospel.

Remission of Sins (Acts x. 43; Heb. x. 18).
Reconciliation to God (2 Cor. v. 20; Rom. v. 10).
Regeneration by the Spirit (Titus iii. 5; 1 Pet. i. 23).

143. Two Conditions of Heart.

A *True* Heart (Heb. x. 22)—Draws near to God.
An *Evil* Heart (Heb. iii. 12)—Departs from God.

144. Prayer.

The Place for Prayer, "Everywhere" (1 Tim. ii. 8).
The Time for Prayer, "Always" (Luke xviii. 1).
Subjects for Prayer, "Everything" (Phil. iv. 6).
Answers to Prayer, "All Things" (Matt. xxi. 12).
Conditions of Prayer, "In My Name" (John xiv. 14).

145. Seven "I Wills" of the Believer.

A Full Confession of Faith.

"I will trust and not be afraid" (Isa. xii. 2).
"I will bless the Lord" (Psa. xxxiv. 11).
"I will love thee, O Lord" (Psa. xviii. 1).
"I will keep thy statutes" (Psa. cxix. 145).
"I will walk before the Lord" (Psa. cxviii. 9).
"I will praise thee" (Psa. cxxxix. 14).
"I will behave myself wisely" (Psa. ci. 2).

146. Christ's Present Work for His People.

He saves them (Rom. v. 10).
He appears for them (Heb. ix. 24).
He makes intercession (Rom. viii. 34).
He keeps them (Jude 24).
He cleanses them (Eph. v. 26).
He restores them (Psa. xxiii. 2).
He leads them (John x. 4).

147.   Jesus Christ Our Object.

Looking unto Jesus (Heb. xii. 2)—Our Example.
Learning of Jesus (Luke x. 39)—Our Teacher.
Leaning on Jesus (Song of Sol. viii. 5)—Our Strength.
Looking for Jesus (Phil. iii. 20)—Our Hope.

148.   A Disciple of Christ.

His Credentials and Character.

His Master (John xiii. 14).
His Book (2 Tim. iii. 16).
His Clothing (1 Pet. v. 5).
His Badge (John xiii. 35).
His Cross (Luke xiv. 27).
His Companions (Psa. cxix. 63).
His Fruit (John xv. 8).

149.   Saints of New Testament Time.

Showing Varied Spiritual Conditions.

Believing Romans (Rom. i. 8).
Progressive Thessalonians (2 Thess. i. 3).
Obedient Philippians (Phil. ii. 12).
Loving Colossians (Col. i. 4).
Faithful Ephesians (Eph. i. 1).
Carnal Corinthians (1 Cor. iii. 3).
Foolish Galatians (Gal. iii. 1).

150.   Union with Christ and One Another.

In Four Aspects.

Members of the Body (Eph. iv. 15-16)—Christ the Head.
Branches in the Vine (John xv. 5)—Christ the Stem.
Stones in the Building (Eph. ii. 20-22)—Christ the Corner.
Sheep of a Flock (Acts xx. 28)—Christ the Shepherd.

151. Christ's Gifts to His People.

He gave His Life (John x. 1-5).
He gave Himself (Gal. ii. 20).
He gives His Spirit (1 John iii. 24).
He gave His Words (John xvii. 8).
He gives His Peace (John xiv. 27).
He gave His Example (John xiii. 15).
He gives His Glory (John xvii. 22).

152. Three Great Changes

In which all Believers Share.

Translated, at Conversion (Col. i. 13; Acts xxvi. 18).
Transformed, by Contemplation (2 Cor. iii. 18; Rom. xii. 2).
Transfigured, at Glorification (Phil. iii. 1; John iii. 2).

153. Five Relations of Believers.

Children in Relationship (1 John i. 12).
Sons in Dignity (Rom. viii. 14).
Priests in Nearness (1 Pet. ii. 5).
Saints in Separateness (Eph. v. 3).
Kings in Authority (Rev. i. 6).

154. Christ the Living One.

A Living Stone (1 Pet. ii. 4 R.V.)—To Rest Upon.
A Living Way (Heb. x. 26)—To Draw Near Through.
A Living Priest (Heb. vii. 25)—To Represent Us.
A Living Hope (1 Pet. i. 3 R.V.)—To Wait For.

155. Obedience to God.

The Proof of Conversion (Rom. vi. 16).
The Recognition of God (Acts v. 29).
The Mark of Children (1 Pet. i. 14).
The Manifestation of Love (John xiv. 15 R.V.).

156.   Four Rests.

Rest to the Conscience (Matt. xi. 28)—In Christ.
Rest for the Heart (Matt. xi. 29)—Under Christ.
Rest amid Service (Mark vi. 30)—With Christ.
Rest in Heaven (Heb. iv. 9)—Like Christ.

157.   Saved.

By God (2 Tim. i. 9)—The Source.
Through Grace (Eph. ii. 5)—The Spring.
In Christ (John x. 9)—The Cause.
By Faith (Luke vii. 50)—The Means.
By Christ Risen (Rom. v. 10)—The Security.
In Hope (Rom. viii. 24)—The Consummation.

158.   Groaning.

The Sinner's Groan (Exod. ii. 24)—For Deliverance.
The Saviour's Groan (John xi. 33)—In Sympathy.
The Spirit's Groan (Rom. viii. 26)—Of Witnessing.
The Saint's Groan (2 Cor. v. 2-4)—For Emancipation.
Creation's Groan (Rom. viii. 22)—For Glory.

159.   The Saint's Sacrifice.

His Praise (Heb. xiii. 15).
His Body (Rom. xii. 1).
His Service (Phil. ii. 17).
His Means (Phil. iv. 18).

160.   The Authority of the Lord Jesus.

The word "Power" is "Authority"—see Rev. Ver.

Over all Flesh (John xvii. 2 R.V.).
In Heaven and on Earth (Matt. xxviii. 18).
To Forgive Sins (Matt. xi. 6 R.V.).
To Execute Judgment (John v. 27).

161. Revival in Three Stages.

"Revive Me" (Psa. cxxxviii. 7).
"Revive Us" (Psa. lxxxv. 6).
"Revive Thy Work" (Hab. iii. 2).
   This is God's order, and must not be reversed.

162. Three Lines of Truth.

Christ Truth, John's Subject (See John i. 1-3, &c.)
Church Truth, Paul's Theme (See Eph. iii. 5-7 &c.)
Kingdom Truth, Peter, James and Jude (1 Pet. ii. 9 &c.)

163. A Triplet in Phil. iv.

Careful for Nothing (Ver. 6)—No Burdens.
Prayerful for Everything (Ver. 6)—No Reserves.
Thankful for Anything (Ver. 6)—No Murmurs.

164. Christ the Beloved.

Accepted in the Beloved (Eph. 1. 6)—Our Place.
Listening to the Beloved (Song of Sol. ii. 8)—Our Attitude.
Leaning on the Beloved (Song of Sol. viii. 5)—Our Dependence.
Speaking of the Beloved (Song of Sol. v. 10-16)—Our Testimony.
Waiting for the Beloved (Song of Sol. viii. 14)—Our Hope.

165. Three Aspects of the Spirit's Work,

In John xvi.

To Glorify God (Verse 14).
To Convict Sinners (Verse 8).
To Instruct Saints (Verse 14).

166. Christ the Shepherd.

The Good Shepherd (John x. 1)—Dying.
The Great Shepherd (Heb. xiii. 20)—Living.
The Chief Shepherd (1 Pet. v. 4)—Coming.

167.   Exhortation.

Let the peace of God rule in your hearts (Col. iii. 15)—Peace.
Let the Word of Christ dwell in you (Col. iii. 16)—Strength.
Let His mind be in you (Phil. ii. 5)—Conformity.
Let your moderation be known unto all (Phil. iv. 5)—Character.
Let your conversation be without covetousness (Heb. xiii. 5)—
    Conduct.
Let your light so shine before men (Matt. v. 16)—Testimony.
Let your loins be girded about (Luke xii. 36)—Watchfulness.

168.   Three Walks.

Before God (Gen. xvii. 1)—Reality.
After God (Deut. xiii. 4)—Obedience.
With God (Gen. v. 22)—Communion.

169.   Seven Aspects of Christian Life.

In 1 Peter, Chapter ii.

Babes (Ver. 2)—Feeding.
Living Stones (Ver. 5)—Builded.
A Holy Priesthood (Ver. 5)—Worshipping.
Strangers (Ver. 11)—Away from Home.
Pilgrims (Ver. 11)—Going Home.
Servants (Ver. 18)—Obeying.
Sufferers (Ver. 20)—Submitting.

170.   In the Heart.

The Love of God shed abroad (Rom. v. 5).
The Peace of God ruling (Col. iii. 15).
Christ Himself indwelling (Eph. iii. 17).

171. The Believer's Feet.

Set on a Rock (Psa. xl. 2)—Salvation.
Cleansed by the Word (John xiii. 10)—Communion.
Kept by Divine Power (1 Sam. ii. 9)—Preservation.
Shod with Peace (Eph. vi. 15)—Warfare.
Running with the Gospel (Rom. x. 15)—Service.
Bruising Satan (Rom. xvi. 20)—Victory.

172. Love in Four Aspects.

The Son's Love to the Father (John xiv. 3).
The Father's Love to the Son (John xv. 9).
The Son's Love to the Saint (John xv. 9).
The Saints' Love to One Another (John xv. 12).

173. Three Offices of the Lord Jesus.

Saviour (Luke ii. 11)—Past.
Priest (Heb. iv. 14)—Present.
Bridegroom (Matt. xxv. 6)—Future.

174. "Stand Fast."

Stand fast in the *Liberty* (Gal. v. 1)—Decision.
Stand fast in the *Faith* (1 Cor. xvi. 11)—Devotion.
Stand fast in the *Lord* (Phil. iv. 1)—Discipleship.
Stand fast in one *Spirit* (Phil. i. 27)—Unity.

175. Christ's Three Gifts.

To All His Redeemed People.

Eternal Life (John xvii. 4).
The Word (John xvii. 14).
The Glory (John xvii. 22).

176.   The Spirit's Threefold Witness.

"He shall bear witness of me" (John xv. 26)—Revelation.
"Ye shall be witnesses unto me" (Acts i. 8)—Declaration.
"Our gospel came in the Holy Ghost" (1 Thess. i. 5)—Attestation.
The *First* is the Spirit's witness *to* us of Christ.
The *Second* the Spirit's witness *through* us for Christ.
The *Third* the Spirit's witness *in* others to Christ.

177.   Satan and the World.

The "Prince" of this world (John xii. 31)—Politically.
The "God" of this world (2 Cor. iv. 4)—Religiously.

178.   Walking Worthy.

Walk worthy of God (1 Thess. ii. 12).
Walk worthy of the Lord (Col. i. 10).
Walk worthy of the Vocation (Eph. iv. 1).

179.   Two Periods.

Fullness of Time (Gal. iv. 4)—The Incarnation.
Fullness of the Times (Eph. i. 10)—The Millennium.
    The former is connected with Christ's Humiliation, the latter with Christ's manifested Glory.

180.   Salvation in Three Aspects.

Saved by Christ's Death (Rom. v. 9)—From Sin's Penalty.
Saved by Christ's Life (Rom. v. 10)—From Sin's Power.
Saved at Christ's Coming (Rom. xiii. 11)—From Sin's Presence.

181.   Three Christ-filled Psalms.

Psa. xxii., The Cross—A Suffering Christ.
Psa. xxiii. The Crook—A Risen Christ.
Psa. xxiv., The Crown—A Reigning Christ.

182. Three Looks.

Backward Look (Isa. xlv. 22—To The Dying One.
Upward Look (Heb. xii. 2)—To The Living One.
Onward Look (Titus ii. 13)—To The Coming One.

183. The Word of God.

Regenerating (1Pet. i. 23).
Feeding (1 Pet. ii. 2).
Sanctifying (John xvii. 17).
Upbuilding (Acts xx. 32).
Enlightening (Psa. cxix. 105).

184. Faith in Varied Stages.

No Faith (Matt. xvi. 8)—The Unbeliever.
Little Faith (Matt. xv. 28)—The Doubter.
Growing Faith (2 Thess. i. 3)—The Healthy Saint.
Strong Faith (Rom. iv. 20)—The Aged Pilgrim.
Full of Faith (Acts vi. 8)—The Fearless Saint.

185. The Believer's Standing and State.

Saved by Christ (2 Tim. i. 9)—His Place.
Sanctified in Christ (1 Cor. i. 2)—His Position.
Separated to Christ (Psa. iv. 3)—His Path.
Satisfied with Christ (Psa. lxiii. 5)—His Portion.
Swift for Christ (Psa. cxlvii. 15)—His Practice.

186. Joy.

In Three Stages of Christian Life.

At Its Beginning (Acts viii. 8-39; xvi. 34; 1 Thess. i. 6).
Throughout Its Course (1 Pet. i. 8; 1 John i. 4).
At Its Close (Acts xx. 24; 2 Tim. iv. 7).

187. The Christian Conflict.

INTERNAL, with the Flesh (Gal. v. 17); not after the flesh (2 Cor. x. 3); with the Armor of Light (Rom. xiii. 12).

EXTERNAL, with the World (John xvi. 33); not by resistance but submission; with the Armor of righteousness (2 Cor. vi. 7).

INFERNAL, with the Devil (Eph. vi. 12); not by submission but resistance (Jas. iv. 7); with the whole Armor of God (Eph. vi. 13).

188. The Believer's Places of Privilege

In Relation to the Lord Jesus.

In His Hand (John x. 28)—Place of Security.
On His Shoulder (Luke xv. 5)—Place of Strength.
In His Bosom (John xiii. 25)—Place of Learning.
At His Feet (Luke x. 39)—Place of Communion.

189. A Threefold Choice

Of All Believers in Christ.

Chosen to Salvation and Glory (2 Thess. ii. 13).
Chosen for Heavenly Provision and Holiness (Eph. i. 4).
Chosen unto Separation and Service (1 Pet. i. 2).

190. The Shadow of His Wings.

Place of Refuge (Psa. lvii. 1).
Place of Security (Psa. xxxvi. 7).
Place of Rejoicing (Psa. lxiii. 7).

191. Two Seekers.

Christ seeking Sinners (Luke xix. 10).
The Father seeking Worshippers (John iv. 23).

192. Key Words to the Four Gospels.

Matthew—"Behold Your King" (John xix. 14).
Mark—"Behold My Servant" (Isa. xlii. 1).
Luke—"Behold The Man" (John xix. 5).
John—"Behold Your God" (Isa. xl. 9).

193. The Service of Christ.

Past—"He came to minister" (Mark x. 45).
Present—"He is a minister of the sanctuary" (Heb. viii. 2).
Future—"He shall come forth and serve" (Luke xii. 37).

194. Sorrow and Joy.

Christ's Exceeding Sorrow (Mark xiv. 34)—In View of the Cross.
Christ's Exceeding Joy (Jude 24)—In Presence of His Glory.

195. The Blessed Man.

As Portrayed in the Psalms.

The Forgiven Man (Psa. xxxiii. 1).
The Trusting Man (Psa. xxxiv. 8).
The Separated Man (Psa. i. 1).
The Disciplined Man (Psa. xciv. 12).
The Obedient Man (Psa. cxii. 1).

196. Three Conditions of Soul.

In Psalm lxiii.

"My soul thirsteth" (Ver. 8)—Desire.
"My soul shall be satisfied" (Ver. 15)—Decision.
"My soul followeth hard" (Ver. 24)—Devotion.

197.   Three Aspects of Faith.

Looking *to* Christ (Isa. xlv. 22)—For Salvation.
Leaning *on* Christ (John xiii. 23)—In Communion.
Living *unt*o Christ (2 Cor. v. 15)—In Service.

198.   Continuing.

In the Love of Christ (John xv. 9).
In the Word of Christ (John viii. 31).
In the Grace of God (Acts xiii. 43).
In the Faith (Acts xiv. 22).
In the Things Learned (2 Tim. iii. 14).

199.   Jesus Christ the Lord.

JESUS—The Saviour (Matt. i. 21)—For Me.
CHRIST—The Anointed (Gal. ii. 20)—In Me.
LORD—The Owner (John xiii. 11)—Over Me.

200.   Walking Worthy.

Of God (1 Thess. ii. 12)—Whose Children we are.
Of the Lord (Col. i. 10)—Whose Servants we are.
Of our Vocation (Eph. iv. 1)—Whose Exponents we are.

201.   The Joy of Angels.

In Creation's Morning (Job xxxviii. 7).
At Christ's Coming (Luke ii. 13).
For a Sinner's Conversion (Luke xv. 10).

202.   Continual Occupation.

Continual Prayer (Acts vi. 4; Col. iv. 2).
Continual Praise (Psa. xxxiv. 1 with Heb. xiii. 15).
Continual Service (Dan. vi. 16-20).

203. Abiding in Christ.

For Fruitfulness (John xv. 4-5).
For Prayer (John xv. 7).
For Confidence (1 John ii. 28).
For Holiness of Walk (1 John iii. 16).
    How to Abide (John vi. 56; 1 John ii. 24-27).

204. "Ready."

To Hear (Eccl. v. 1)—Discipleship.
To Do (2 Sam. xv. 15)—Service.
To Preach (Rom. i. 15)—Testimony.
To Die (Acts xxi. 13)—Devotedness.
    This order is the true path of Christian life and testimony.

205. Instruments of Divine Discipline.

The Word (2 Tim. iii. 16)—For Correction and Instruction.
The Knife (John xv. 2)—For Pruning and Fruitfulness.
The Thorn (2 Cor. xii. 7)—For Prevention and Power.
The Rod (Heb. xii. 5-7)—For Chastisement and Punishment.

206. "No Difference."

In Sin and Need (Rom. iii. 22).
In Salvation and Acceptance (Rom. x. 12).
In Standing and Liberty (Acts xv. 9).

207. Triune Love.

The Love of God (Rom. v. 8).
The Love of Christ (Rom. viii. 35).
The Love of the Spirit (Rom. xv. 30).

208.   Three Good Men.

A Good Man (Acts xi. 24)—Right with God.
A Good Minister (1 Tim. iv. 6)—Ready for God.
A Good Steward (1 Pet. iv. 10)—True to God.

209.   Three Great Truths

In the Epistle to the Romans.

No Condemnation, in Christ (Rom. viii. 1).
No Separation, from Christ (Rom. viii. 35).
No Reservation, for Christ (Rom. xii. 1).

210.   "His Own Blood."

For our Purchase (Acts xx. 28).
For our Loosing from Sin (Rev. i. 5 R.V.).
For our Sanctification (Heb. xiii. 12).

211.   Emblems of the Holy Spirit.

Wind (Acts ii. 2; John iii. 8)—To Awaken.
Breath (Ezek. xxxvii.)—To Give Life.
Water (Ezek. xlvii. 2-13)—To Cleanse and Heal.
Oil (Psa. xxiii. 5; 1 John ii. 20)—To Anoint and Enlighten.

212.   Seven "One Anothers."

Which produce and maintain true "fellowship one with another."

Receive one another (Rom. xv. 7).
Esteem one another (Phil. ii. 3).
Consider one another (Heb. x. 24).
Edify one another (Rom. xiv. 19).
Exhort one another (Heb. iii. 13).
Admonish one another (Rom. xv. 14).
Submit to one another (Eph. v. 21).

213. "To the Lord."

Turned to the Lord (Acts ix. 35)—Conversion.
Added to the Lord (Acts v. 14)—Fellowship.
Living to the Lord (Rom. xiv. 8)—Devotion.
Cleaving unto the Lord (Acts xi. 23)—Discipleship.
Making Melody to the Lord (Col. iii. 16)—Worship.
Doing it heartily to the Lord (Col. iii. 23)—Service.

214. The Believer Has in Heaven:

A Saviour (Phil. iii. 20).
An Inheritance (1 Pet. i. 4).
His Name written there (Luke x. 20).
His Citizenship is there (Phil. iii. 20).
His Hope laid up (Col. i. 5).
His Master is there (Eph. vi. 9).
His Home is there (Heb. xi. 16).

215. A Threefold Ministry.

Wooing and Winning (Prov. xi. 30)—The Evangelist.
Watering and Watching (Heb. xiii. 17)—The Pastor.
Witnessing to and Warning (Col. i. 28)—The Teacher.

216. What Is God Able To Do?

Able To Save (Heb. vii. 25).
Able To Keep (2 Tim. i. 12).
Able To Deliver (Dan. iii. 17).
Able To Succor (Heb. ii. 18).
Able To Subdue (Phil. iii. 21).

217. Our God.

God *for* us (Rom. viii. 31)—Justifying.
God *with* us (Gen. xxviii. 15)—Keeping.
God *in* us (1 John iv. 16)—Indwelling.

218. Christ's Threefold Headship.

Head of Creation (Col. i. 15-17)—Eternally.
Head of Every Man (1 Cor. xi. 3)—Federally.
Head of His Body (Col. i. 18)—Vitally.

219. Abiding in Christ.

We bear much fruit (John xv. 5).
We do not actively sin (1 John iii. 6).
We await His coming (1 John ii. 28).

220. Things To "Hold Fast."

The Name (Rev. ii. 13).
The Word (Titus i. 9).
The Hope (Heb. x. 23 R.V.).
That which is good (1 Thess. v. 21).
How?—"In Faith and Love" (2 Tim. i. 13).
How Long?—"Till I Come" (Rev. ii. 25).

221. The Christian's Hope

is not the uncertain thing of men, but the well grounded expectation of that which God hath prepared for and promised to His people.

It is Christ in them (Col. i. 27).

A Good Hope (2 Thess. ii. 16).
A Living Hope (1 Pet. i. 3).
A Purifying Hope (1 John iii. 3).
A Blessed Hope (Titus ii. 13).

222. The Seal and Earnest.

The Seal (Eph. ii. 13)—Securing Believers for Heaven.
The Earnest (Eph. i. 14)—Ensuring Heaven to them.

The former marks God's claim on them; the latter their claim on God.

223. All Things

In Relation to the Lord Jesus.

He is *before* all things (Col. i. 17).
By Whom are all things (Heb. ii. 10).
For Whom are all things (Heb. ii. 10).
Heir of all things (Heb. i. 2).
Pre-eminent in all things (Col. i. 18).
He will *fill* all things (Eph. iv. 10).

224. Three Great Facts

In Ephesians, Chapter i.

Chosen by God the Father (Verse 4).
Redeemed by God the Son (Verse 7).
Sealed by God the Spirit (Verse 13).

225. In Christ Jesus

The Believer Has

Salvation (2 Tim. ii. 10).
Sanctification (1 Cor. i. 2).
Preservation (Jude 1).
Glorification (2 Thess. i. 12).

226. The Church in Three Aspects.

A Building (Chap. ii. 20-21)—Christ the Foundation.
A Body (Chap. iv. 15-16)—Christ the Head.
A Bride (Chap. v. 25-32)—Christ the Bridegroom.

227. Sowing.

What to Sow—"Precious Seed" (Psa. cxxvi. 6).
How to Sow—"In Tears" (Psa. cxxvi. 6).
Where to Sow—"Beside all Waters," (Isa. xxxii. 20).
When to Sow—"Morning," "Evening," always (Eccl. xi. 6).

228.   "Before the Foundation."

The Son beloved of the Father (John xvii. 24).
The Lamb foreordained to die (1 Pet. i. 20).
The Church chosen in Christ (Eph. i. 4).

229.   Three Great Truths

In 1 Peter 1.

Redemption gives a New Owner (Verse 18).
Resurrection brings to a New Position (Verse 19).
Regeneration imparts a New Life (Verse 23).

230.   Three Graces

In 1 Thessalonians Chapter i.

"Work of *Faith*" (Ver. 3)—Turned to God (Ver. 9).
"Labour of *Love*" (Ver. 3)—Serve the Living God (Ver. 9).
"Patience of *Hope*" (Ver. 3)—Wait for the Son (Ver. 10).

231.   Three Classes of Workers

In Nehemiah Chapter iii.

"Who put not their necks" (Ver. 5)—Honorary.
"Who repaired the wall" (Ver. 6)—Practical.
"Who repaired earnestly" (Ver. 20)—Devoted.

232.   The Believer's Place and Portion.

On His Shoulder (Luke xv. 5)—Our Salvation.
In His Hand (John x. 28)—Our Security.
At His Feet (Luke x. 39)—For Teaching.
On His Bosom (John xiii.)—In Communion.

233. Continuing.

Continue in the Grace of God (Acts xiii. 43).
Continue in the Faith (Acts xiv. 22).
Continue in the Things Learned (1 Tim. iii. 14).
Continue in the Love of Christ (John xv. 9).
Continue in Prayer (Col. iv. 2).

234. The Christian in Varied Aspects.

A Child in RELATIONSHIP (1 John iii. 1).
A Saint in SEPARATION (Rom. i. 7).
A Priest in NEARNESS (1 Pet. iii. 5).
A Steward in RESPONSIBILITY (1 Pet. v. 10).
A Witness in TESTIMONY (Acts xxvi. 16).

235. Present Blessings.

Now, justified by His blood (Rom. v. 8)—Justification.
Now, delivered from the law (Rom. vii. 6)—Deliverance.
Now, no condemnation (Rom. viii. 1)—Freedom.
Now, made nigh (Eph. ii. 13)—Nearness.
Now, the sons of God (1 John iii. 1)—Sonship.

236. The False.

The Devil's Counterfeits of God's Realities.

False Christs (Matt. xxiv. 24, with 1 John ii. 18).
False Apostles (Rev. ii. 2, with 2 Cor. xi. 13).
False Teachers (2 Pet. ii. 1, with 2 Tim. iii. 8).
False Brethren (Gal. ii. 4, with 2 Cor. xi. 26).

237. The Hope of the Believer.

A Living Hope (1 Pet. i. 3).
A Good Hope (2 Thess. ii. 16).
A Blessed Hope (Titus ii. 13).
A Purifying Hope (1 John iii. 3).

238.   Full Assurance.

Full Assurance of Faith (Heb. x. 22).
Full Assurance of Understanding (Heb. vi. 11).
Full Assurance of Hope (Col. ii. 2).
Faith rests in Christ's finished work—Past.
Understanding learns Christ's place—Present.
Hope looks onward to Christ's glory–Future.

239.   Good Things for God's People.

To draw near to God (Psa. lxxiii. 28).
To give thanks (Psa. xcii. 1).
To bear the yoke (Lam. iii. 27).
To be afflicted (Psa. cxix. 71).
To be zealously affected (Gal. iv. 8).

240.   God and Father.

To Christ (John xx. 17; 1 Pet. i. 3; Eph. iii. 14).
To Christians (Eph. iv. 6; Gal. iv. 6; Eph. i. 17).

In these two great relationships does God stand to Christ, and to us, and such are the names by which saints should address Him.

241.   God and His People.

God *for* His people (Rom. viii. 31)—Saving.
God *with* His people (Gen. xxxiii. 15)—Keeping.
God *in* His people (2 Cor. vi. 16)—Dwelling.

242.   A Fourfold Relation to Christ.

My Sheep (John x. 27)—In Security.
My Disciples (John xv. 8)—In Obedience.
My Friends (John xv. 14)—In Communion.
My Brethren (John xx. 17)—In Relationship.

243. **The Bible.**

"The Holy Scriptures" (2 Tim. iii. 15)—Divine Inspiration.
"The Oracles of God" (Rom. iii. 2)—Divine Authority.
"The Word of God" (Matt. vii. 36)—Divine Revelation.

244. **God Manifested in Christ.**

"God was manifest in the flesh" (1 Tim. iii. 16).
The Word of Life (1 John i.)—God Heard.
The Light of Life (John viii. 12)—God Seen.
The Fullness of Life (John x. 10)—God Enjoyed.

245. **Paul's Five Faithful Sayings.**

Salvation (1 Tim. i. 15).
Service (1 Tim. iii. 1).
Suffering (1 Tim. iv. 7).
Recompense (2 Tim. ii. 11).
Testimony (Titus iii. 8).

246. **The Inheritance and Its Heirs.**

The Saints' inheritance prepared for them (1 Pet. i. 4).
The Saints made meet for the inheritance (Col. i. 12).

247. **Tears.**

Tears of Faith (Mark ix. 24).
Tears of Devotion (Luke vii. 38).
Tears of Service (Acts xx. 19).
Tears of Sympathy (2 Tim. i. 4 R.V.)
Tears of Warning (Acts xx., 31 R.V.)

248. **The Word of God.**

Converts (Psa. xix. 7)—The Soul.
Enlightens (Psa. xix. 8)—The Eyes.
Cleanses (Psa. cxix. 9)—The Ways.

249.   Paul's Growth.

In Three Stages, at Three Dates.
A.D. 59—The Least of the Apostles (1 Cor. xv. 9).
A.D. 64—Less than the Least of Saints (Eph. iii. 8).
A.D. 66—The Chief of Sinners (1 Tim. i. 15).

250.   The Believer's Standing.

Standing in Grace (Rom. v. 2).
Standing by Faith (2 Cor. i. 24).
Standing Fast in Liberty (Gal. v. 1).
Standing in Armor of God (Eph. vi. 11).

251.   Christ Set Down.

As Described in the Epistle to the Hebrews.

As Sin Purger (Chap. 1).
As Great High Priest (Chap. viii. 1).
As Perfecter of Faith (Chap. xii. 2).

252.   Christ the Fullness.

The Father's Pleasing (Col. i. 19).
In Christ all fullness dwells (Col. ii. 9).
Of His fullness we received (John i. 16).
The Church the fullness of Christ (Eph. i. 23).

253.   Three Deaths.

In which all Believers share, true of all judicially in Christ,
actually to faith.

Dead to the Law (Rom. vii. 4).
Dead to the World (Col. ii. 20).
Dead to Sin (Rom. vi. 2).

254. Three Stages of Progress in Communion.

As set forth in the Song of Songs.

"My Beloved is Mine and I am His" (ii. 16).
"I am My Beloved's and My Beloved is Mine" (vi. 13).
"I am My Beloved's, His desire toward Me" (vii. 10).
The *First* is what I have in Him—Foremost.
The *Second* is what He has in me—First.
The *Third* is, Him only—Mine forgotten.

255. Threefold Cleansing.

Our Consciences (Heb. x. 2-22)—By the Blood.
Our Ways (Psa. cxix. 9)—By the Word.
Ourselves (2 Cor. vii. 1)—By Separation.

256. Three Favored Disciples.

Peter, James, and John, thrice taken by the Lord apart.

To See His Power (Mark v. 37)—In Jairus' House.
To Share His Sorrow (Mark xiv. 33)—In the Garden.
To Behold His Glory (Mark ix. 2)—On the Mount.

257. "In My Name."

Salvation in My Name (Acts iv. 12).
Service in My Name (Mark ix. 41).
Praying in My Name (John xiv. 13).
Gathering in My Name (Matt. xviii. 20).
Holding Fast My Name (Rev. ii. 13).

258. Following the Lord.

Obediently as a Sheep (John x. 27).
Devotedly as a Servant (John xii. 26).
Patiently as a Sufferer (1 Pet. ii. 21).

259.   Christ Manifested.

As Set Forth in John's First Epistle.

Manifested as the Life (1 John i. 2)—In His Life.
Manifested to take away Sins (1 John iii. 5)—In His Death.
Manifested in Glory (1 John iii. 2)—At His Appearing.

The word in each case is the same, and occurs nine times in 1 John.

260.   God's Fourfold Testimony to Christ.

God anointed Him (Acts x. 38)—At His Baptism.
God was with Him (Acts x. 38)—In His Service.
God raised Him (Acts xiii. 30)—From the Grave.
God ordained Him (Acts xvii. 31)—As the Judge.

261.   A Sevenfold View of the Spirit's Work.

As Seen in Ephesians.

The Seal of the Spirit (Chap. i. 13).
The Earnest of the Spirit (Chap. i. 14).
The Revealing of the Spirit (Chap. i. 17).
Access by the Spirit (Chap. ii. 18).
Strength of the Spirit (Chap. iii. 16).
Fullness of the Spirit (Chap. v. 18).
Praying in the Spirit (Chap. vi. 17).

262.   Three "Togethers."

For All Servants of Christ.

Praying Together (Acts iii. 1)—One Desire.
Working Together (2 Cor. vi. 1)—One Master.
Striving Together (Phil. i. 27)—One Aim.

263.   **Eternal Life.**

In Three Different Aspects.

A Promise (Titus i. 4)—Past.
A Possession (1 John v. 9)—Present.
A Prospect (Rom. vi. 22)—Future.

264.   **The Word Applied Daily.**

To Search the Inner Man (Heb. iv. 12).
To Sanctify the Outward Walk (John xvii. 17).
To Cleanse the Way (Psa. cxix. 9).
To Feed the New Life (1 Pet. ii. 2).

265.   **The Work of Grace in the Believer.**

As shown in the Philippian Epistle.

The Work Begun (Chap. i. 6)—Inauguration.
The Work Progressing (Chap. ii. 13)—Progression.
The Work Completed (Chap. iii. 21)—Consummation.

266.   **Three Fundamental Truths.**

In Hebrews x.

The Will of God (Verse 7)—The Source.
The Work of Christ (Verse 10)—The Cause.
The Witness of the Spirit (Verse 15)—The Seal.

267.   **The Lord's Body.**

Prepared by the Father (Heb. x. 5).
Taken at Incarnation (Heb. ii. 14).
Offered at Calvary (Heb. x. 10).
Buried in the Tomb (John xix. 40).
Handled in Resurrection (Luke xxiv. 39).
Glorified at Ascension (Phil. iii. 21 R.V.)
Discerned in Communion (1 Cor. xi. 29).

268.   Christ's Service for the Church.

In Seven Particulars (Eph. v. 25-27).

He Loved the Church. } Past:
He Gave Himself.   } At the Cross.

He Sanctifies.
He Cleanses.   } Present:
He Nourishes.   } On the Throne.
He Cherishes.

He Will Present.   } Future:
                      } At Its Coming.

269.   Threefold Cords.

In Which the Names of the Three Persons of the Godhead Appear.

In Atonement (Heb. ix. 14).
In Resurrection (Rom. viii. 11).
In Regeneration (John i. 12; 1 John v. 1; John iii. 5).
In Prayer (Rom. viii. 27).
In Union (Eph. ii. 22).

270.   Preparation for Service.

Of the Servant (2 Tim. ii. 21; Exod. xxxv. 30-35-36).
Of the Heart (Ezra vii. 10; 1 Sam. viii. 3).
Of the Message (Eccl. xii. 10, with 2 Tim. iii. 18).

271.   In Adam and in Christ.

By our connection in Nature with Adam, we inherit the sin; by union with Christ through grace we receive the grace.

IN ADAM.	IN CHRIST.
Sin (Rom. v. 12).	Righteousness (2 Cor. v. 21).
Condemnation (Rom. v. 19).	Justification (Rom. iv. 25).
Death (Rom. v. 23).	Life (1 John v. 11).

272. **The Christian Warrior.**

And His Panoply in Eph. vi. 13-18.

Girdle of Truth (Ver. 14, with Psa. li. 6; Col. iii. 16).
Breastplate of Righteousness (Ver. 14, with Prov. xxviii. 1).
Sandals of Peace (Ver. 15; Rom. v. 1, x. 15).
Shield of the Faith (Ver. 16; Psa. xci. 4; Jude 3).
Helmet of Salvation (Ver. 16; Psa. xxvii. 1; Eph. ii. 8).
Sword of the Spirit (Ver. 17; Heb. iv. 12; Matt. iv. 7).

273. **Spiritual Hygiene.**

Pure Milk (1 Pet. ii. 2; Heb. v. 13).
Healthy Food (1 Tim. vi. 3, iv. 6).
Strict Cleanliness (Psa. cxix. 9; Eph. v. 26).
Plenty of Exercise (1 Tim. iv. 7; Heb. xii. 11).

274. **What Christ Does for His People.**

He Quickens them (John v. 25)—As the Life Giver.
He Saves them (Matt. i. 21)—As the Saviour.
He Seals them (Eph. i. 13)—As the Owner.
He Leads them (John x. 27)—As the Shepherd.
He Succors them (Heb. ii.)—As the Priest.
He Restores them (1 John ii. 1)—As the Advocate.
He Comes for them (John xiv. 3)—As the Bridegroom.

275. **Seven Togethers with Christ.**

Which Bind the Saints Indissolubly to Him.

Crucified Together (Rom. vi. 5-6; Gal. ii. 20).
Buried Together (Rom. vi. 4; Col. ii. 12).
Quickened Together (Eph. ii. 5; Col. ii. 13).
Raised Together (Eph. ii. 6; Col. iii. 1).
Seated Together (Eph. ii. 6; Rev. iv. 4).
Sufferers Together (Rom. viii. 17; 1 Pet. iv. 13).
Glorified Together (Rom. viii. 18; 2 Tim. ii. 12).

276.   **"The Faith."**

Once grace delivered to the Saints (Jude 3, R.V.)

One newly come to the Faith (1 Tim. iii. 6).
One weak in the Faith (Rom. xiv. 1).
One who kept (guarded) the Faith (2 Tim. iv. 7).
Some who erred from the Faith (1 Tim. vi. 21).
Some depart from the Faith (1 Tim. iv. 1).
Some deny the Faith (1 Tim. v. 8).
Some overthrow the Faith (2 Tim. ii. 18).

277.   **Scriptural Arithmetic.**

As Exemplified in the Early Church.

ADDITION—Three Thousand Added (Chap. ii. 41).
SUBTRACTION—Two Taken Away (Chap. v. 1-10).
MULTIPLICATION—Disciples Multiplied (Chap. vi. 1).
DIVISION—Scattered Abroad (Chap. viii. 1).

278.   **Joy.**

In Christ (John xv. 11).
In the Spirit (Rom. xiv. 17).
In God (Rom. v. 11).

279.   **Seven Links with the Lord.**

Knowing the Lord (Heb. viii. 11).
Confessing the Lord (Rom. x. 9).
Following the Lord (Josh. xiv. 8).
Serving the Lord (Acts xx. 19).
Honoring the Lord (Prov. iii. 9).
Magnifying the Lord (Psa. xxxiv. 3).
Present with the Lord (2 Cor. v. 8).

280.   God's Attributes Toward Us.

Mercy shown toward us (Psa. lxxxvi. 13).
Kindness manifested toward us (Eph. ii. 7).
Love commended toward us (Rom. v. 8).
Grace abounding toward us (2 Cor. ix. 8).

281.   God's First Things.

Seek ye *first* the Kingdom of God (Matt. vi. 33).
Cleanse *first* that which is within (Matt. xxiii. 26).
First cast out the beam out of thine own eye (Matt. vi. 6).
Learn *first* to show piety at home (1 Tim. v. 4).
Judgment must *first* begin at house of God (1 Pet. iv. 17).

282.   Christ the Living One.

The Living STONE on which we *build* (1 Pet. ii. 5).
The Living BREAD on which we *feed* (John vi. 51).
The Living WAY by which we draw *near* (Heb. x. 20).
The Living PRIEST through whom we *worship* (Heb. xiii. 25).
The Living HOPE for which we *wait* (1 Pet. i. 3).

283.   Good Works.

The Believer in Christ Is

Created unto good works (Eph. ii. 10).
Furnished unto all good works (2 Tim. iii. 17).
Careful to maintain good works (Tit. iii. 8).
Prepared unto every good work (2 Tim. ii. 21).
Zealous of good works (Tit. ii. 14).
Rich in good works (1 Tim. vi. 18).
A Pattern in good works (Tit. ii. 7).

284.   The Lord's Death.

As described by Himself.

For the Sheep (John x. 11).
For the Many (Matt. xx. 28).
For the World (John vi. 51).

285.   Symbols of the Word.

A *Mirror* to show us ourselves (Jas. i. 23).
A *Hammer* to break the will (Jer. xxiii. 29).
A *Fire* to melt the heart (Jer. xxiii. 29).
A *Sword* to pierce the conscience (Heb. iv. 12).
A *Seed* to quicken the soul (1 Pet. i. 23).
A *Laver* to cleanse the way (Eph. v. 26).
A *Light* to show the path (Psa. cxix. 105).

286.   Characteristics of God's Word.

The Word of Life (Phil. ii. 16)—To Be Held Forth.
The Word of Reconciliation (2 Cor. v. 19)—Proclaimed.
The Word of Salvation (Acts xxviii. 26)—To Be Heard.
The Word of Truth (Eph. i. 13)—To Be Received.
The Word of Faith (Rom. x. 8)—To Be Believed.
The Word of Wisdom (1 Cor. xii. 8)—To Be Ministered.
The Word of Faithfulness (Tit. i. 9)—To Be Held Fast.

287.   Threefold Peace.

Perfect Peace (Isa. xxvi. 3).
Abundant Peace (Jer. xxx. 6).
Peace passing all understanding (Phil. iv. 7).

288.   The Believer's Offerings.

His Body (Rom. xii. 1)—Acceptable.
His Praises (Heb. xiii. 15)—Well Pleasing.
His Gifts (Phil. iv. 18)—Sweet Smelling.

289.   **Christ the Deliverer.**

Read Rom. xi. 26; Luke i. 74; Luke iv. 18.

He delivers all His people from—

The Lowest Hell (Psa. lxxxiv. 12; Rev. xx. 15).
The Wrath To Come (1 Thess. i. 10; Rom. viii. 1).
The Power of Darkness (Col. i. 13; 1 Pet. ii. 9).
The Curse of Law (Rom. vii. 6; Gal. ii. 19).
The Present World (Gal. i. 3; John xvii. 16).
The Power of Evil (2 Tim. iii. 11, iv. 17).
The Presence of Sin (Rom. viii. 21; 1 John iii. 2).

290.   **Our Great High Priest.**

Called in Resurrection (Heb. v. 7, with Acts xiii. 33).
Acting in Heaven (Heb. iv. 4, viii. 1, ix. 24).
Character and Work (Heb. ii. 17, iv, 15, vii. 26).
Order and Dignity (Heb. vi. 20, vii. 4, 17, 24, 28).

291.   **The Power of Love.**

Drawn by Love (Jer. xxxi. 3)—In Conversion.
Satisfied by Love (Song of Sol. ii. 4)—In Communion.
Constrained by Love (2 Cor. v. 14)—In Consecration.
Energized by Love (Phil. i. 17)—In Confession.

292.   **The Blood of Christ.**

Procures for Believers

Remission of sin (Matt. xxvi. 28; Acts x. 38).
Reconciliation to God (Col. i. 20; 2 Cor. v. 21).
Redemption from Bondage (Eph. i. 7; 1 Pet. i. 19).
Justification from sin (Rom. v. 9, iii. 25).
Nearness to God (Eph. ii. 13; Heb. x. 19).
Fitness for Heaven (Rev. vii. 14, v. 9).

293.   Christ in His People.

Christ liveth in me (Gal. ii. 20)—Their Life.
Christ dwelling in them (Eph. iii. 17)—Their Strength.
Christ in you the Hope (Col. i. 27)—Their Hope.

294.   Fruits of Regeneration.

Love to God and His People (1 John v. 2, iv. 7).
Victory over the World (1 John v. 4, ii. 16).
Doth not practice sin (1 John iii. 9, v. 18 R.V.).
Lives a righteous life (1 John ii. 29).

295.   Four Views of Christ.

The Son of God (John i. 49, xx. 31).
The Son of Man (Luke ix. 22, xix. 10).
The Sacrifice for Sin (Heb. ix. 22, x. 12).
The Saviour of Sinners (1 Tim. i. 15; Rom. v. 8).

296.   Four Views of Man.

Created in God's Image (Gen. i. 27; Eccl. vii. 29).
Ruined by Sin (Rom. v. 12; Rom. iii. 12).
Regenerated by the Spirit (John iii. 7; Eph. iv. 24).
Conformed to Christ (Rom. viii. 29; 2 Thess. i. 10).

297.   Three Great Realities.

Sin has ruined all (Rom. iii. 23).
Christ has ransomed all (1 Tim. ii. 6).
Faith saves all (Acts xiii. 39).

298.   The Name of Jesus.

The Power To Save (Matt. i. 21).
The Channel of Life (John xx. 31).
The Means of Remission (Acts x. 43).
The Center of Gathering (Matt. xviii. 20).

299. **Three Relationships.**

In John's Gospel.

"My Sheep" (John x. 14)—Christ the Shepherd.
"My Friends" (John xv. 14)—Christ the Lover.
"My Brethren (John xx. 17)—Christ the Firstborn.

300. **Living.**

The Living God (1 Thess. i. 9)—To Serve.
The Living Christ (1 Pet. ii. 5)—To Come to.
The Living Word (Heb. iv. 12)—To Search us.
The Living Bread (John vi. 51)—To Feed on.
The Living Way (Heb. x. 20)—To Draw Near by.
The Living Water (John iv. 10)—To Drink.
The Living Sacrifice (Rom. xii. 1)—To Offer.

301. **Two Classes To "Mark."**

"Mark them which so walk" (Phil. iii. 17).
"Mark them that cause divisions" (Rom. xvi. 17-18).
The former are godly *walkers;* the latter godless *talkers.*

302. **The Bodies of Christ.**

The Body of His Flesh (Col. i. 22)—Christ Human.
The Body of His Glory (Phil. iii. 21 R.V.)—Christ Glorified.
His Body the Church (Col. i. 18)—Christ Mystical.

303. **The Christian Calling.**

In Its Threefold Character.

A High Calling (Phil. iii. 14, with 1 Sam. i. 8).
A Heavenly Calling (Heb. iii. 1, with Eph. i. 3).
A Holy Calling (2 Tim. i. 9, with 1 Pet. i. 15 R.V.)

304. The Christian Race.

Running after Christ (Song of Sol. i. 4).
Running in His Way (Psa. cxix. 32).
Running with Patience (Heb. xii. 1).
Running, not uncertainly (1 Cor. ix. 26).
Running, yet not weary (Isa. xl. 31).
Running, looking unto Jesus (Heb. xii. 2 R.V.)

305. Seeing Jesus.

"We *would* see Jesus" (John xii. 21)—An Earnest Desire.
"We *do* see Jesus" (Heb. ii. 9)—An Open Vision.
"We *shall* see Jesus" (1 John iii. 2)—A Bright Prospect.

306. Rejoicings.

God the Father rejoicing (Zeph. iii. 17).
God the Son rejoicing (Luke xv. 6).
The Church rejoicing (Acts xv. 3).
The Servant rejoicing (Phil. iv. 10).
The Saved Sinner rejoicing (Luke xv. 24).

307. Things To Learn.

For All Young Believers.

Learn of Christ (Matt. xi. 28)—Inner Life.
Learn to keep the Word (Psa. cxix. 71)—Social Life.
Learn to show Piety (1 Tim. v. 4)—Home Life.
Learn to do Well (Isa. i. 17)—Church Life.
Learn to maintain Good Works (Titus iii. 14)—World Life.

308. The Christian in the World.

As a Saint (John xvii. 16)—In Separation from it.
As a Subject (Rom. xiii. 1)—In Subjection to it.
As a Servant (John xx. 21)—In Service toward it.

309. **Keeping.**

Keep thine heart (Prov. iv. 23).
Keep thyself pure (1 Tim. v. 22).
Keep yourselves unspotted (James i. 27).
Keep yourselves in the Love of God (Jude 21).

310. **The Kingdom of God.**

A Spiritual Sphere, Created and Governed by God.

Natural Man cannot see or enter it (John iii. 3-5; 1 Cor. vi. 9).
Its Origin, through the Word (Mark iv. 26; 1 Pet. i. 23).
Its Character and Development (Rom. xiv. 17; 1 Cor. iv. 20).
To Be Sought after First (Matt. vi. 23; Acts xiv. 22).
True Ministry furthers it (Acts xx. 25; xxviii. 23; Col. iv. 11).

311. **The Heart and Its Inmates.**

The Heart in Nature (Jer. xvii. 9-10; Matt. xv. 18).
The Heart at Conversion (2 Cor. iv. 6; Acts xvi. 14; Rom. x. 9).
The Heart's New Dwellers (Gal. iv. 6; Eph. iii. 17; Psa. cxix. 11).
The Heart's New Motive (Rom. v. 4; 1 Pet. i. 22; Matt. xii. 35).
The Heart's New Condition (Heb. x. 22; Matt. v. 8; Eph. v. 19).

312. **Three Appearings of Christ.**

Hebrews ix. 24-28.

"He once appeared" (Verse 26)—Atonement.
"He now appears" (Verse 24)—Advocacy.
"He shall appear" (Verse 28)—Advent.

313. **Two Periods.**

"Latter Times" (1 Tim. iv. 1)—Romanism and Ritual.
"Last Days" (2 Tim. iii. 1)—Rationalism and Religion.

314. Disciples of Christ.

The Gospel's Object (Matt. xxxiii. 18)—"Make Disciples."
The Apostles' Practice (Acts xiv. 21)—"They made Disciples."
The True Marks (John xiii. 35; Luke xiv. 26)—Love, Obedience.
The Plain Path (Matt. x. 24-25; Luke xiv. 27)—Rejection.

315. The Love of Christ.

To His Father (John xiv. 31, with Exod. xxi. 5).
To His Church (Eph. v. 25; Rev. iii. 9).
To His Saints (Rev. i. 5; John xi. 5).
To the Individual (Gal. ii. 20; John xiv. 23).

316. Gathering.

Gathering to Christ by the Gospel (John xii. 32).
Gathering to Christ, in the Church (Matt. xviii. 20).
Gathering to Christ at His Coming (2 Thess. ii. 1).

317. Three Fellowships.

The Fellowship of Life (1 John i. 2-3).
The Fellowship of Light (1 John i. 7).
The Fellowship of Labor (Phil. iv. 3).

318. "The Saints."

Saints called by Grace (Rom. i. 7).
Saints gathered to Christ (Psa. l. 5).
Saints in Assembly (Psa. lxxxix. 7).
Saints faithfully Ruled (Hos. xi. 12).
Saints glorified with Christ (2 Thess. i. 10).

319. The Believer's Justification.

The *Source* of Justification (Rom. viii. 33)—God.
The *Principle* of Justification (Rom. iii. 24)—Grace.
The *Cause* of Justification (Rom. v. 8)—Blood.
The *Way* of Justification (Rom. v. 1)—Faith.
The *Proof* of Justification (Jas. ii. 18)—Works.

320. The Death of Christ.

In Seven Aspects.

A Death of Shame (Heb. xii. 2; Isa. l. 6; Mark xiv. 65).
A Death of Suffering (Luke xxii. 15; Heb. ii. 9-10).
A Martyr's Death (1 Pet. ii. 21; Acts ii. 23; xiii. 28).
A Sacrificial Death (Heb. ix. 14; Eph. v. 2; Heb. ix. 26).
A Sin-bearing Death (1 Pet. ii. 24; Isa. liii. 6; John i. 29).
A Voluntary Death (John x. 18; xviii. 8-11; xiv. 21).
An All-Sufficient Death (John xiv. 30; Heb. i. 2; Isa. xlii. 21).

321. The Taker-away of Sin.

(John i. 29).

By Sacrifice (Heb. ix. 26)—From Before God.
By Salvation (Matt. i. 21)—From His People.
By Sanctification (1 John iii. 9)—In His Saints.

322. Four Attitudes of Believers.

As Seen at the Close of the Four Gospels.

As Worshippers *of* Christ (Matthew xxviii. 9).
As Workers *with* Christ (Mark xvi. 19).
As Witnesses *to* Christ (Luke xxiv. 47).
As Waiters *for* Christ (John xvi. 22).

323. The Christian's Race.

The Start (Heb. xii. 1)—Conversion and Stripping.
The Course (1 Cor. ix. 24)—From the Cross to Glory.
The Goal (Phil. iii. 12)—Christ in Glory.
The Reward (2 Tim. iv. 8; 1 Cor. ix. 25)—A Crown.

324. Christ Is All.

As Sacrifice (Heb. x. 12-18)—No Romanism.
As Priest (Heb. viii. 1)—No Ritualism.
As Lord (1 Cor. viii. 7)—No Lawlessness.
As Head (Col. ii. 19)—No Clerisy.
As Object (Phil. iii. 14)—No Worldliness.

325. Vessels.

Marred in the Fall (Jer. xviii. 3-4, with Eph. ii. 10).
Chosen by Grace (Acts ix. 15; Eph. i. 4).
Prepared for Glory (Rom. ix. 23; Rev. xxi. 11).
Fitted for Service (2 Tim. ii. 21; iii. 17).

326. Three Aspects of the Holy Spirit's Work.

Regenerating (John iii. 5, with Titus iii. 5).
Indwelling (John iv. 14, with Rom. viii. 14-15).
Outflowing (John vii. 38, with Gal. iii. 5).

327. Christian Earnestness.

Give earnest heed to the Word (Heb. ii. 1).
Earnestly contend for the Faith (Jude 3).
Earnestly pray to God (Luke xxii. 24; Jas. v. 17).
Earnest care for saints (2 Cor. vii. 7).
Earnest longing for glory (2 Cor. v. 2).

328. Meekness.

Receive the Word with meekness (Jas. i. 21)—Inwardly.
Be clothed with meekness (Col. iii. 12)—Outwardly.
A meek and quiet spirit (1 Pet. iii. 4)—Manifestly.
Restoring the erring with meekness (Gal. v. 1)—In Service.
Answer every man in meekness (1 Pet. iii. 15)—In Testimony.

329. Four Links with Christ.

In the Colossian Epistle.

Quickened with Christ (Chap. ii. 13).
Risen with Christ (Chap. iii. 1).
Hid with Christ (Chap. iii. 3).
Appearing with Christ (Chap. iii. 4).

330. God's Little Things.

A Little Flock (Luke xii. 32)—To Care for.
A Little Strength (Rev. iii. 8)—To Serve.
A Little While (Heb. x. 37)—To Wait.

331. "Go's" of Christ.

Go and *Sell* (Mark x. 21)—To the Rich one.
Go and *Tell* (Mark v. 19)—To the Saved one.
Go and *Shew* (Luke xvii. 14)—To the Cleansed one.
Go and *Teach* (Matt. xxviii. 18)—To the Sent one.

332. Christian Postures.

Sitting as a Learner (Luke x. 39).
Kneeling as a Suppliant (Acts xx. 36).
Leaning as a Weakling (Song of Sol. viii. 5).
Standing as a Warrior (Eph. vi. 14).
Running as a Racer (Heb. xii. 1).

333.   **Objects To Consider.**

In the Epistle to the Hebrews.

Consider the Apostle and High Priest (Chap. iii. 1).
Consider Him who endured (Chap. xii. 3).
Consider one another (Chap. x. 24).

334. **A Threefold Work of the Spirit.**

Described in Romans viii.

The Spirit of Life (Ver. 2)—Giving Freedom.
The Spirit of Sonship (Ver. 14)—Giving Guidance.
The Spirit of Intercession (Ver. 26)—Giving Help.

335.   **Three Crucifixions.**

In Galatians vi. 14-16.

Of Christ—"The Cross of Our Lord Jesus."
Of the World—"The World Crucified to Me."
Of Self—"I to the World."

336.   **Things Everlasting.**

The Present Possession of All Believers.

Everlasting Love (Jer. xxxi. 3).
Everlasting Life (John vi. 47).
Everlasting Salvation (Isa. xlv. 17).
Everlasting Strength (Isa. xxvi. 4).

337.   **The Presence of the Lord.**

Is Intolerable to the Sinner (Gen. iii. 8; iv. 16).
Is Salvation to the Saint (Psa. xlii. 5 marg; xxxi. 8).
Is Rest to the Servant (Exod. xxxiii. 14-15).

338. Three Kinds of Giving.

Thanksgiving (Eph. v. 20; Heb. xiii. 15).
Substance-giving (2 Cor. ix. 7; Heb. xiii. 16).
Self-giving (2 Cor. viii. 5; Rom. vi. 13).

339. Seven Aspects of Christian Life

In 2 Timothy, Chap. ii.

A Son (Ver. 1)—In Affection.
A Steward (Ver. 2)—In Faithfulness.
A Soldier (Ver. 2)—In Endurance.
A Wrestler (Ver. 5)—In Skill.
A Workman (Ver. 15)—In Diligence.
A Vessel (Ver. 21)—In Fitness.
A Servant (Ver. 24)—In Obedience.

340. "In Love."

Walking in Love (Eph. v. 2).
Acting in Love (Eph. iv. 2).
Speaking in Love (Eph. iv. 2).

341. Three Requests of the Lord Jesus.

"Watch with Me" (Mark xii. 37).
"Remember Me" (1 Cor. xi. 24).
"Follow Me" (John xxi. 19).

342. Three States of the Believer.

In 2 Cor. v. 1-8.

In our "Earthly House" (Ver. 1)—The Present State.
"Unclothed" (Ver. 4)—The Intermediate State.
"Clothed Upon" (Ver. 2)—The Eternal State.

343. Names Given to God's People in "Acts."

Believers (Acts v. 14)—In Faith.
Brethren (Acts vi. 3)—In Love.
Disciples (Acts ix. 1)—In Obedience.
Saints (Acts ix. 3)—In Separation.
Christians (Acts xi. 26)—In Testimony.

344.   Christian Liberality.

How To Give (2 Cor. ix. 7; Rom. xii. 8).
When To Give (1 Cor. xvi. 2; 2 Cor. ix. 5).
What To Give (1 Cor. ix. 7; 1 Pet. iv. 11).
To Whom To Give (3 John 5-8; Gal. vi. 6).

345.   Enduring Hardness

In 2 Timothy.

[The Greek Word is the same in each case.]

Endure Hardness, in the Gospel (Chap. i. 8).
Endure Hardness, as a Soldier (Chap. ii. 3).
Endure Hardness, unto Bonds (Chap. ii. 9).
Endure Hardness, as an Evangelist (Chap. iv. 5).

346.   Three Great Foes.

The World (James iv. 4)—Around us.
The Flesh (Gal. v. 17)—Within us.
The Devil (Eph. vi. 11-12)—Above us.

347.   Prayer, Praise, Worship.

In *Prayer* we are occupied with our *Needs* (Mark xi. 24).
In *Praise* we are rejoicing in our *Fullness* (Psa. lii. 9).
In *Worship* we are occupied with our *God* (John iv. 24).

348. Acceptable Service.

Serve with all thine heart (Deut. x. 12).
Serve with a willing mind (1 Chron. xxviii. 9).
Serve with all humility (Acts xx. 19).
Serve with gladness (Psa. c. 2).

349. Threefold Glory of God.

His Creation Glory (Psa. xix. 1)—In the Heavens.
His Redemption Glory (2 Cor. iv. 4)—In Christ Risen.
His Eternal Glory (1 Pet. v. 10)—In His Saints.

350. "For the Name."

Forsaking all for the Name (Matt. xix. 29).
Going forth for the Name (3 John 8).
Laboring for the Name (Rev. ii. 3).

351. Christ the Girded Servant.

In the Upper Room (John xii. 4)—Past.
In the Midst of the Churches (Rev. i. 13)—Present.
In the Coming Glory (Luke xii. 37)—Future.

352. Spiritual Progress.

From Faith to Faith (Rom. i. 7).
From Strength to Strength (Psa. lxxxiv. 7).
From Glory to Glory (2 Cor. iii. 18).

353. Two Washings in John xiii. 10.

"He that is *washed*," washed all over—Once for all.
"*Wash* his feet," wash in part—Continuously.
The *first* accords with the washing of Regeneration (Tit. iii. 4).
The *second* with the daily cleansing by the Word (Psa. cxix. 9).

354.   Seal and Earnest of the Spirit.

(Ephesians i. 13-14).

God's *Seal,* marking His claim upon us.
Our *Earnest,* the pledge and foretaste of Glory.

355.   Three Leavens.

Leaven of Pharisees (Matt. xvi. 1)—Ritualism.
Leaven of Sadducees (Luke xvi. 11)—Rationalism.
Leaven of Herod (Matt. viii. 15)—Lawlessness.

356.   Fruitfulness.

"Fruit" (John xv. 2)—By Union.
"More Fruit" (John xv. 2)—By Pruning.
"Much Fruit" (John xv. 5)—By Abiding.

357.   Daily Fare for a Weakly Believer.

The Roast Lamb (Exod. xii. 9)—Christ Crucified.
The Daily Manna (Luke xv. 23)—Christ Humbled.
The Old Corn (Josh. v. 11)—Christ Glorified.
New Wine (John ii. 10)—Heavenly Joy.
Pure Milk (1 Pet. ii. 2)—The Word.
Grapes of Eschol (Numb. xiii. 23)—The Spirit's Earnest.

358.   "Jesus in the Midst."

Among the Doctors (Luke ii. 46)—Hearing.
On the Cross (John xix. 18)—Suffering.
Among the Disciples (John xx. 19-29)—Comforting.
In the Assembly (Matt. xviii. 20)—Gathering.
Among the Churches (Rev. i. 13)—Judging.
In the Glory (Heb. ii. 12)—Singing.
On the Throne (Rev. v. 6)—Reigning.

359. Three "Abides."

"Abide *with* Me" (1 Sam. xxii. 23)—Safety.
"Abide *in* Me" (John xv. 4)—Communion.
"Abide *for* Me" (Hosea iii. 3)—Stewardship.

360. Our God.

God *Before* us (Deut. i. 30).
God *Behind* us (Isa. lii. 12).
God *Above* us (Psa. xviii. 16).
God *Underneath* us (Deut. xxxiii. 27).
God *Around* us (Psa. cxxv. 2).

361. The Christian a Soldier.

His Captain (Heb. ii. 10; Josh. v. 14).
His Comrades (Phil. ii. 26; Philem. 2).
His Armor (Eph. vi. 11-18).
His Enemy (1 Pet. v. 8; Eph. vi. 12).
His Fight (1 Tim. vi. 12; i. 18).

362. Man's History.

Man Created in God's Image (Gen. i. 27).
Man Ruined by Sin (Rom. v. 12).
Man Redeemed by Christ (Eph. i. 7).
Man Regenerated by the Spirit (John iii. 5).
Man Rejoicing in Hope of Glory (Rom. v. 2).

363. How To Use the Word.

Search it (John v. 39; 1 Pet. i. 10-11).
Examine it (Acts xvii. 11; 1 Cor. ii. 10-13).
Meditate in it (Psa. i. 2; cxix. 15).
Delight in it (Psa. cxix. 47; Jer. xv. 17).
Declare it (Psa. cxix. 13; Jer. xxiii. 28).

364.   Seven "In Whoms"

In the Epistle to the Ephesians.

In whom we have Redemption (Chap. i. 7).
In whom we trusted (Chap. i. 13).
In whom believing we are sealed (Chap. i. 13).
In whom we have inheritance (Chap. i. 11).
In whom we are builded together (Chap. ii. 22).
In whom the building is framed together (Chap. ii. 21).
In whom we have access (Chap. iii. 12).

365.   Three Persons of the Godhead,

In Romans, Chapter viii.

God our Justifier (Verses 31-32).
Christ our Intercessor (Verses 34-35).
The Spirit our Helper (Verses 26-27).

366.   Two Pointed Questions.

"Who art thou that judgest another?" (Jas. iv. 12).
"Who is sufficient for these things?" (2 Cor. ii. 16).

367.   Two Doors.

The Closed Door (Matt. vi. 6)—For Prayer.
The Opened Door (Rev. iii. 8)—For Service.

368.   "Shall Nots."

True of All Believers in Christ.

Shall not perish (John x. 28).
Shall not come into judgment (John v. 24).
Shall not want (Psa. xxiii. 1).
Shall not be afraid (Psa. cxii. 7).
Shall not walk in darkness (John viii. 12).

369.   Threefold Victory.

Victory over Sin (Rom. vi. 14-15)—By the Gospel.
Victory over Satan (1 John ii. 13-14)—By the Word.
Victory over the World (1 John v. 4-5)—By Faith.

370.   Jehovah's Wings.

Wings of shelter (Psa. xvii. 8).
Wings of security (Psa. xci. 4).
Wings of support (Deut. xxxii. 11).

371.   Tongues.

Confounded at Babel (Gen. xi. 8)—Judgment.
Preaching at Pentecost (Acts ii. 6)—Grace.
Praising in Heaven (Rev. v. 9)—Glory.

372.   Christ the True,

As set forth in John's Gospel.

The True Light (John i. 9)—Receive Him.
The True Bread (John vi .32)—Feed on Him.
The True Vine (John xv. 1)—Abide in Him.

373.   Four Attitudes in Ephesians.

Seated with Christ (Chap. ii. 6).
Kneeling in Prayer (Chap. iii. 14).
Walking in Love (Chap. v. 2).
Standing in Armor (Chap. vi. 13).

374.   Threefold Judgment.

As Sinners (Gal. ii. 20; John v. 24)—Past.
As Saints (1 Cor. xi. 31, 32; 1 Pet. v. 19)—Present.
As Servants (2 Cor. v. 9; 1 Cor. iii. 13-15)—Future.

375.   Boldness.

Boldness to draw near to God (Heb. x. 19).
Boldness to speak the Word (Acts vi. 31).
Boldness in the Judgment (1 John iv. 17).

376.   Three Divine Provisions,

For all the Lord's People.

The Will of the Lord (Jas. v. 14)—Our Guide.
The Way of the Lord (Acts xviii. 25)—Our Path.
The Work of the Lord (1 Cor. xv. 58)—Our Business.

377.   Things We Are To "Find."

REST under the Yoke *of* Christ (Matt. xi. 29).
PASTURE by going in and out *with* Christ (John x. 9).
GRACE by drawing near *to* Christ (Heb. iv. 16).

378.   Angelic Joy.

At Creation (Job xxvii. 7).
At Incarnation (Luke ii. 13).
At Conversion (Luke xv. 10).

379.   The Believer's Body.

A *Member* of Christ (1 Cor. vi. 15).
A *Temple* of the Spirit (1 Cor. vi. 19).
A *Sacrifice* to God (Rom. xii. 1).

380. The Believer in Three Relations.

Upright in his relation to God (Prov. xiv. 2).
Unspotted in his relation to the World (Jas. i. 27).
Unblameable in his relation to the Church (1 Thess. ii. 10).

381. **A Busy Chapter.**

(Acts xii.)

Persecution of the Saints (Verses 1-4).
Prison for the Servant (Verses 5-11).
Prayer of the Church (Verses 12-17).
Preservation by the Lord (Verses 17-23).
Progress of the Word (Verse 24).
Pride and its Punishment (Verses 21-23).

382. **Bible Houses.**

House of Bondage (Deut. vii. 8; viii. 14).
House of Salvation (Exod. xii. 7, 13, 27).
House of Instruction (Deut. vi. 7; xi. 19).
House of Communion (Song of Sol. ii. 4; Psa. lxxxiv. 4).
House of Reunion (John xiv. 2).

383. **Four Cardinal Truths.**

Redemption (Eph. i. 7)—For the Slave.
Reconciliation (Rom. v. 10)—For the Enemy.
Regeneration (Titus iii. 5)—For the Sinner.
Restoration (Gal. vi. 1)—For the Wanderer.

384. **What We Wait For.**

Waiting for the Coming of the Lord (1 Cor. i. 7).
Waiting for the Redemption of the Body (Rom. viii. 23).
Waiting for the Manifestation of the Sons of God (Rom. viii. 19).

385. **Effectual Prayer.**

In the Name of Christ (John xiv. 13-14).
In the Holy Ghost (Jude 20).
In Faith (Jas. i. 6); Heb. xi. 6).

386. Light.

Our Enlightenment (2 Cor. iv. 6)—Light in us.
Our Environment (1 Pet. ii. 9)—We into light.
Our Employment (Eph. v. 8)—Walk in light.
Our Equipment (Rom. xiii. 12)—Armor of light.

387. Laying on of Hands.

In Blessing (Gen. xlviii. 14-20; Mark x. 16).
In Judgment (Lev. xxiv. 15; Deut. xvii. 7).
In Impartation (Acts viii. 17; xix. 6).
In Fellowship (Acts xiii. 3).

388. The Rock.

Of Salvation (2 Sam. xxii. 47).
Of Shelter (Psa. lxi. 2).
Of Refreshment (1 Cor. x. 4).

389. Three Remarkable Days.

Day of Salvation (2 Cor. vi. 2).
Day of Redemption (Eph. iv. 30).
Day of Judgment (2 Pet. ii. 9).

390. Good Security.

"*No* weapon formed against you shall prosper" (Isa. liv. 17).
"*Nothing* shall by any means hurt you" (Luke x. 19).
"*No one* is able to pluck you" (John x. 28).

391. Prayer.

Personal (Eph. i. 16; iii. 14).
Social (Acts xii. 12).
Church (Acts ii. 42; xii. 5).

392. Pride.

Pride of Race (John viii. 33)—National.
Pride of Place (James ii. 2-3)—Social.
Pride of Face (James i. 24)—Personal.
Pride of Grace (1 Tim. vi. 4)—Spiritual.

393. John's Four Sights of Christ.

"We beheld his glory" (John 1. 14).

At the Transfiguration (Mark ix. 7).
At the Crucifixion (John xix. 26).
At the Resurrection (John xxi. 20).
In the Revelation (Rev. i. 16-17).

394. "Take Heed."

"What ye hear" (Mark iv. 24)—The Matter.
"How ye hear" (Luke viii. 18)—The Manner.
"How you build" (1 Cor. iii. 10)—The Work.

395. Three "Walks."

Our Old Walk (Eph. ii. 3)—Past.
Our New Walk (Rom. vi. 4)—Present.
Our Future Walk (Rev. iii. 4)—Prospective.

396. Three Seals.

The Father's Seal on the Son (John vi. 37).
The Believer's Seal on the Word (John iii. 33).
The Spirit's Seal on the Saint (Eph. i. 13).

397. Giving.

God gave His Son (John iii. 16).
Christ gave Himself (Gal. ii. 20).
Believers give themselves (2 Cor. viii. 5).

398.   The Faithfulness of God.

In Cleansing from Sin (1 John i. 9).
In Delivering from Temptation (1 Cor. x. 13).
In Keeping from Evil (2 Thess. iii. 3).
In Sanctifying Wholly (1 Thess. v. 24).

399.   Striving.

The word in all these Texts is the same throughout, and might
be uniformly translated "agonize."

In Prayer (Col. iv. 12).
In Conflict (2 Tim. iv. 7).
In Ministry (Col. i. 29).
In Running (1 Cor. ix. 25).

400.   "With One Accord."

In Prayer (Acts i. 14; iv. 24).
In Hearing the Word (Acts viii. 6).
In Gathering Together (Acts ii. 46; v. 12).
In Peace and Unity (Acts xv. 25).

401.   Things To "Buy."

Wine and milk (Isa. lv. 1)—For Salvation.
The Truth (Prov. xxiii. 23)—For Sanctification.
Gold tried in the fire (Rev. iii. 18)—For Preservation.

402.   "I Come Quickly."

Three times in Rev. xxii.

"I come quickly" (Ver. 7)—To the Disciple.
"I come quickly" (Ver. 12)—To the Servant.
"I come quickly" (Ver. 20)—To the Bride.

403. Warning Words.

Beware of Covetousness (Luke xii. 15)—The Heart.
Beware of Men (Col. ii. 8)—The Mind.
Beware of False Teachers (2 Pet. iii. 17)—The Path.

404. Three Looks.

Looking *to* the Saviour (Isa. xlv. 22)—Salvation.
Looking *on* the Master (John i. 36)—Contemplation.
Looking *for* the Bridegroom (Titus ii. 13)—Glorification.

405. Baptismal Truths.

The Baptism of John (Matt. iii. 6)—Repentance.
The Baptism of the Cross (Luke xii. 50)—Judgment.
The Baptism of the Spirit (1 Cor. xii. 13)—Unity.
The Baptism of Believers (Rom. vi. 4)—Identification.

406. Baptism.

Believers are the Subjects (Acts vi. 41; viii. 12).
Immersion is the Mode (Matt. iii. 16; Acts viii. 38).
Burial is the Meaning (Rom. vi. 4; Col. ii. 12).

407. The Lord's Supper.

Its Institution (Matt. xxvi. 26-28).
Its Celebration (Acts xx. 7; 1 Cor. xi. 23).
Its Meaning (1 Cor. x. 16; xi. 24-26).

CHURCH TRUTHS

408. Two Aspects of the Church.

The Body of Christ (1 Cor. xii. 12-13)—Of Living Members.
The Temple of God (1 Pet. ii. 5)—Of Living Stones.
Christ is HEAD over the Body.
Christ is FOUNDATION of the Temple.

409. The Church Locally.

Composed of Believers (1 Cor. 1-2; 1 Thess. i. 1-9).
Gathered unto the Name (Matt. xviii. 20; 1 Cor. v. 4).
Governed by the Lord (1 Cor. xii. 3-5).
Guided by the Spirit (1 Cor. xii. 7-8; Phil. iii. 3 R.V.).
Ordered by the Word (1 Cor. xi. 23; xii. 36-37).

410. The Church's Constitution.

Matthew xviii. 20.

"Where"—A Divine Location.
"Two or three"—A Divine Testimony.
"Are Gathered"—A Divine Drawing.
"Together"—A Divine Unity.
"In My Name"—A Divine Authority.
"There am I"—The Divine Presence.
"In the midst of them"—The Divine Center.

411. "Churches of the Saints."

Composed of Saints by Calling (Rom. i. 7; Eph. i. 1).
Commended by Saintly Character (Philemon i. 5-17; Rom. xvi. 2
Characterized by Saintly Conduct (Rom. xii. 13; Eph. v. 3; Heb.
    vi. 10).
Constituted by Faith delivered to the Saints (Jude 3).

412.   The Church Prospectively.

A Mystery to be Revealed (Eph. iii. 3-9).
A Pearl to be Purchased (Matt. xiii. 45-46).
A Building to be Begun (Matt. xvi. 17-18).

413.   Four Figures of the Church.

A House for God (1 Tim. iii.)—To Rule.
A Body for Christ (Eph. i. 23)—To Supply.
A Temple for the Spirit (Eph. ii.)—To Indwell.
A Lampstand to the World (Rev. ii., iii.)—To Give Light.

414.   The Church in Four Epochs.

In the Purpose of God (Eph. i. 4; Titus i. 2).
Purchased at the Cross (Eph. v. 26; Acts xx. 28).
Formed by the Spirit (1 Cor. xii. 13; Eph. iv. 4).
Presented in Glory (Eph. v. 27; Jude 24).

415.   The Church at Ephesus.

Its Formation (Acts xviii. 9).
Its Instruction (Eph. i.-vi.)
Its Watching (1 Tim. i. 3).
Its Danger (Acts xx. 17-29).
Its Inspection (Rev. i. 13; ii. 1-7).

416.   The Church's Pattern.

The Master Builder's Instructions (1 Cor. iii. 10; xi. 1).
The Architect's Pattern (1 Cor. xi. 2, 23; 1 Tim. iii. 15).
The Proper Materials (1 Cor. iii. 12; 1 Pet. ii. 5).
The Way To Build (Eph. iv. 13; Phil. ii. 1).

417.   Receiving to Church Fellowship.

Whom to Receive—"Saints" (Rom. xiv. 1; Matt. xviii. 5).
How to Receive—"In the Lord" (Rom. xvi. 2; Philemon 15-17; Phil. ii. 29).
Who are to Receive?—"Ye" (Rom. xv. 6-7).
To What are they Received?—"The Fellowship" (Acts ii. 42-44; ix. 28).
Whom to Avoid (Rom. xvi. 18; Titus iii. 10; 2 Tim. iii. 5).

418.   A Good Church Condition.

As seen in Acts ix. 31.

Rest from Persecution or Strife outwardly (1 Cor. xiv. 33).
Edification, built up, inwardly (Eph. iv. 16).
Ministry, in the Spirit unhindered.
Walk, in the fear of the Lord.
Multiplication, growth from within.

419.   Seven Links of Fellowship.

Gathered Together (Matt. xviii. 20).
Framed Together (Eph. ii. 21).
Builded Together (Eph. ii. 22).
Knit Together (Col. ii. 2).
Perfectly joined Together (1 Cor. i. 10).
Striving Together (Phil. i. 27).
Caught up Together (1 Thess. iv. 17).

420.   The Church Corrupted.

FROM WITHIN by	FROM WITHOUT by
Evil Doctrine (1 Tim. i. 20).	Unconverted Professors (Jude 4).
Perverse Things (Acts xx. 30).	False Teachers (2 Peter ii. 1).
False Brethren (Gal. ii. 4).	Many Antichrists (1 John ii. 18).
Proud Men (John iii. 9).	Fables Taught (2 Tim. iv. 4).
Indifference (Rev. ii. 20).	Amalgamation with World (Rev. ii. 13).

421. Seven Fellowships.

Fellowship with the Father (1 John i. 3).
Fellowship of the Son (1 Cor. i. 9).
Fellowship of the Spirit (Phil. ii. 1).
Fellowship in the Light (1 John i. 7).
Fellowship of suffering (Phil. iii. 10).
Fellowship in service (Col. iv. 7).
Fellowship in the Gospel (Phil. i. 3).

422. The Seven Churches.

A History of the entire Church through the age.
Revelation ii., iii.

Ephesus, the Church in early purity.
Smyrna, the Church in Persecution
Pergamos, the Church united with the World.
Thyatira, Romanism ruling supreme.
Sardis, Protestantism.
Philadelphia, the Faithful few.
Laodicea, the World-Church.

The last four go on together until the end.

423. Worship and Worshippers.

What Worship is (Matt. ii. 11; xxviii. 9; 1 Cor. xiv. 25).
Who are Worshippers (John iv. 23; 1 Pet. ii. 9; Phil. iii. 3).
The Place of Worship (Heb. ix. 20; Eph. ii. 18).
The Power for Worship (Phil. iii. 3, R.V.; John iv. 24).

Worship ascends from saints, *in* the Spirit, *through* Christ, *to* the Father.

424.   Ministry.

Christ Glorified (Eph. iv. 8-11)—Its Source.
The Spirit (1 Cor. xii. 4)—Its Administrator.
Edification (Eph. iv. 11)—Its Object.
  Ministry comes *from* God, *through* Christ, *in* the Spirit, *to* the Church.

425.   Rule.

The Holy Spirit the Creator of it (Acts xx. 28).
The Marks of True Rulers (1 Tim. iii. 1-7).
The Duty of owning them (1 Thess. v. 12).

426.   Discipline.

Its Necessity and Object (1 Tim. v. 20).
Its Internal Form (2 Thess. iii. 6-14).
Its Extreme Measure (1 Cor. v. 11-13).
Its Object, Restoration (2 Cor. ii. 7).

427.   Fellowship of Churches.

In Mutual Recognition (Acts xviii. 27; Rom. xvi. 1).
In Service and toward Servants (Acts xi. 22; xiii. 3).
In Substance and Suffering (2 Cor. viii. 1; Acts xi. 29).

TEXTS

428.   **The Great Deliverance.**

Galatians i. 3-4.

The Giver—"Our Lord Jesus Christ."
The Gift—"Himself."
The Object—"For *our* Sins."
The End—"Deliverance from the World."

429.   **Asa's Prayer.**

2 Chron. xiv. 11.

It was Earnest—"He Cried."
It was Personal—"To God."
It was Definite—"Help us."
It was Believing—"We rest on Thee."
It was Answered—Verses 12-15.

430.   **The Believer's History.**

Deuteronomy xxxii. 10.

"Found," with Luke xv. 4-5—A Lost Sinner.
"Led," with John x. 4-28—A Loving Follower.
"Instructed," with Luke x. 39—A Lowly Disciple.
"Kept," with 1 Peter 1. 5—A Living Saint.

431.   **The Exaltation of Christ.**

(Isaiah lii. 13-15).

"Exalted"—At His Ascension (Acts ii. 33, v. 31).
"Extolled"—In His Glory (Rev. iv. 11; v. 12-14).
"Very High"—In His Kingdom (Rev. xix. 16).
    All the words in the Hebrew, signify majesty and power.

432. Faithful Witnesses in Difficult Places.

NOAH in a Godless World (2 Pet. ii. 5).
JOSEPH, in an Officer's House (Gen. xxxix. 2-9).
DAVID, in a King's Palace (1 Sam. xvi. 14-23).
DANIEL, in a Heathen Court (Dan. i. 8).
MORDECAI, in an Enemy's Presence (Esther ii. 1-6).

433.   The Footsteps of the Flock.

Song of Solomon, Chap. i. 7-8.

An Appeal to the Shepherd (Isa. xl. 11).
A Rested Flock (Psa. xxiii. 2; Jer. vi. 16).
Rival Shepherds (1 Cor. i. 12-13, iii. 4-6).
A Gracious Answer (Psa. xxv. 9, xxvii. 9).
A Plain Path (Acts ii. 41-47).
Feeding and Leading (John xxi. 15; 1 Pet. v. 2).

434.   Burden Bearing.

Galatians vi. 2-5.

"Bear one another's burdens" (ver. 2).

Sharing in sorrow, in sympathy, in trial—Fellowship of saints.

"Every man shall bear his own burden" (ver. 5).

Personal and individual responsibility, which must be borne by each, like a ship bringing its cargo into port—Individual Responsibility.

435.   Weary and Unweary.

Isaiah xl. 28-31.

The Unfailing and Unwearying God (Ver. 29).
Fainting and Wearying Man (Ver. 30).
The Waiting Soul Renewed (Ver. 31).
Strength Imparted to Mount up (Ver. 31).
Run unwearied, Walk unfainting (Ver. 31).

436. ## Benjamin's Blessing.

(Deut. xxxii. 12).

True of all the Lord's "little ones" (Gen. xliv. 20).
"The Beloved of the Lord" (Rom. i. 7; Col. iii. 12).
"Dwell in safety, by Him" (Psa. xci. 1; Acts xi. 23).
"Cover him all day long" (Psa. xci. 4, lxxxiv. 11).
"Dwell between His shoulders" (1 Pet. i. 5; Jude 24).

437. ## Downward and Upward.

(Isaiah xxxvii. 31).

"Root Downward"—The Hidden Life, as set forth in Psa. i. 3;
Jer. xvii. 7-8; John xv. 1-6; Jude 21.
"Fruit Upward"—The Manifested Life as described in Rom. vii.
4; Eph. v. 9; Gal. v. 22; Rom. vi. 22; Phil. i. 11.

THE SECOND ADVENT

438. The Personal Return of Christ.

The Lord's Own Promise (John xiv. 3, with Heb. x. 36-37).
A Personal Return (Acts i. 11, with Rev. xxii. 12).
The Lord Himself (1 Thess. iv. 16; Rev. xxii. 17).
The Christian's Hope (1 Tim. i. 1; 1 John iii. 3).

439. The Believer's Attitude.

Waiting for His Coming (1 Cor. i. 7; 1 Thess. i. 10).
Looking for that Blessed Hope (Titus ii. 13; Phil. iii. 20).
The Sleeping Saints, with Christ (Phil. i. 23; 2 Cor. v. 8).
The Living Saints waiting for Christ (Rev. xxii. 20).
Its Practical Power (1 John iii. 3; 1 Thess. iii. 13).

440. Christ's Coming for His Saints.

The Lord Descends to the Air (1 Thess. iv. 16).
The Dead in Christ are Raised (1 Cor. xv. 20-25).
The Living Saints are Changed (1 Thess. iv. 17).
Incorruptibility given the Dead (1 Cor. xv. 52).
Immortality given to the Living (1 Cor. xv. 54).
Caught up Together (1 Thess. iv. 17).
Received by Him (John xiv. 3).

441. The Gathering and Presentation.

Gathered Together unto Him (2 Thess. ii. 1).
Welcomed to the Father's House (John xiv. 2, xvii. 24).
Presented, the Church Glorious (Eph. v. 27).
Presented faultless in Glory (Jude 24).
Crowned in Heaven (Rev. iv. 4-10, v. 6-9).

442. The Judgment Seat of Christ.

The Master's Promise (Rev. xxii. 12; Luke xix. 13).
The Reckoning Day (Matt. xxv. 19; 1 Cor. iv. 5).
The Manifestation of Works (2 Cor. v. 10; Col. iii. 24-25).
Motives and Manner (1 Cor. iv. 5; 2 Tim. ii. 5).
Reward and Loss (1 Cor. iii. 13; 1 Cor. ix. 24-26).
Crowns and Castaways (2 Tim. iv. 8; 1 Pet. v. 4).

443. The Marriage of the Lamb.

A Scene in Heaven (Rev. xix. 7).
The Bride Prepared (Rev. xix. 7; 2 Cor. xi. 2).
The Guests Invited (Rev. xix. 9, with John iii. 29).
The Joy in Heaven (Rev. xix. 7; Jude 24).
The Bride's Attire (Rev. xix. 8, R.V.)

444. The Manifestation in Glory.

CALLED THE "APPEARING" OR "EPIPHANY."
To be distinguished from the *Parousia*, or "Coming."

The Manifestation of Christ in Glory (Titus ii. 13).
With All His Saints (Col. iii. 4; Rev. xix. 11-16).
In Public Glory (Matt. xxiv. 30; Rom. viii. 19).
To Overthrow His Foes (2 Thess. i. 7-10; Jude 14).
To Establish His Kingdom (Zech. xiv. 4-9; Matt. xvii. 4).

445. The Day of the Lord.

A Period of Judgment (Isa. ii. 12-21; 2 Pet. iii. 10).
It will come suddenly (1 Thess. v. 2; Rev. iii. 3).
Judgment on Christ rejecters (2 Thess. i. 8-10, ii. 7-12).
Destruction of Antichrist (2 Thess. ii. 6-8; Rev. xix. 20).
Judgment of Apostate Christianity (Rev. xvii. xviii.)
Satan cast into the Abyss (Rev. xx. 3).

446.   Restoration of Israel.

The Promises of God (Rom. xi. 26; Isa. xi. 11-12).
Conviction and Conversion (Zech. xii. 9-14, xiii. 1).
Return to their Land (Isa. xi. 12, xiv. 1-2; Amos ix. 9).
Reunion of the Tribes (Ezek. xx. 33-38; Isa. lxvi. 20).
The Earthly City (Psa. xlviii. 2, cxxii. 1; Zech. xiv. 8).
The Center of Government (Mic. iv. 2; Jer. xxxiii. 16).

447.   The Millennium.

The Reign of Christ Predicted (Isa. xxxii. 1; Luke i. 32).
Its Postponement (Luke xix. 14; Matt. xxiii. 38-39).
Its Certain Fulfillment (Psa. lxxii. 1; Heb. i. 8).
Its Characteristics (Isa. xi., xxxv.; Rev. xx. 6).
Its Blessings (Psa. lxxii. 5-8; Isa. ii. 4).
Its Heavenly Sphere (Rev. xx. 4; xxi. 10-27).
Its Earthly Aspect (Rom. viii. 20-21; Isa. xi. 9).

448.   The Final Judgment.

Satan Loosed (Rev. xx. 7-8). His Doom (Rev. xx. 10).
The Last Great Rebellion (Rev. xx. 9-27).
The Heavens and Earth Pass Away (2 Pet. iii. 10).
The Dead are Raised (John v. 25-29; Rev. xx. 12).
The Judge on the Throne (Rev. xx. 11; Acts xvii. 31).
The Open Books (Rev. xx. 12; Rom. ii. 16; Rev. iii. 5).
The Final Doom (Rev. xx. 15; xxi. 8; Mark ix. 48).

449.   The Eternal State.

A New Heaven and Earth (Rev. xxi. 1-5; 2 Pet. iii. 13).
The New Jerusalem (Rev. xxi. 1-4, xxii. 1-5).
The Eternal Glory of Christ and His People (1 Pet. v. 10).
God Dwelling with Men (Rev. xxi. 3; Eph. ii. 21).
God, "All in All" (1 Cor. xv. 25).

BIBLE STUDIES

450.   **Life, Light, Liberty.**

The Word received gives *Life* (John v. 24).
The Word entering gives *Light* (Psa. cxix. 108).
The Truth known gives *Liberty* (John viii. 32).

451.   **God's Joy.**

In His People's Salvation (Luke xv. 24).
In His People's Obedience (3 John 4).
In His People's Glorification (Jude 24).

452.   **The Two Natures.**

The Old (Rom. vii. 18; viii. 18; Eph. iv. 22).
The New (1 John iii. 9; Eph. iv. 26).
The Conflict (Gal. v. 17; Rom. vii. 25).
The Way of Victory (Rom. viii. 2-13; Gal. v. 16-25).

453.   **Gospel Service**

In Three Aspects.

"Trustees" (1 Thess. ii. 4)—To Guard it.
"Stewards" (1 Cor. ix. 7)—To Administer it.
"Ambassadors" (2 Cor. v. 20)—To Present it.

454.   **A Threefold Ministry.**

Ministers of God (2 Cor. vi. 4; 1 Thess. iii. 2).
Ministers of Christ (2 Cor. xi. 23; Col. i. 7).
Ministers of the Word (Acts vi. 4; 2 Tim. iv. 4).

455.　　　**Key Words in Ephesians.**

"In Christ" (Chap. i. 3)—Standing.
"In the Lord" (Chap. vi. 1)—Subjection.
"In the Spirit (Chap. v. 18 R.V.)—Condition.
"In one Body (Chap. ii. 16)—Unity.

456.　　　**Lamps and Light**

As a Candle in the Home (Luke xi. 33-36).
As a Lamp in the Church (Rev. i. 12).*
As a Star in the World (Rev. i. 16; ii. 1-20).
　　*The word here is Lampstand (not Candlestick). Believers
are the Lamps, the Church the Lampstand.

457.　　　**A Threefold Possession**

(1 Cor. iii. 22-23).

"All are yours" (Eph. i. 3; Rom. viii. 32; 1 Tim. vi. 17).
"Ye are Christ's (1 Cor. vi. 20; Mark ix. 41).
"Christ is God's" (Matt. iii. 17; Heb. i. 5; Psa. ii. 7).

458.　　　**The Great Commission.**

Matt. xxviii. 18-20.

The Master's Authority (Ver. 18, with John xvii. 2).
The Servant's Commission (Ver. 19, with Mark xv. 15).
The Making of Disciples (Ver. 19, with Acts xiv. 21 mar.).
The Baptizing of them (Ver. 19, with Acts x. 48).
Teaching them all things (Ver. 20, with Acts xiv. 28).
The Promised Presence (Ver. 20, with Acts xi. 21).

459.　　　**Words to Shepherds.**

1 Thessalonians v. 12-14.

A Threefold Work among the Healthy (Ver. 12).
Three Classes of Lame and Feeble (Ver. 14).
A Threefold Service toward such (Ver. 14).

460. ## Four "Alls"

In Matthew xxviii. 18-20.

"All Authority" given to the Lord Jesus.
"All Nations," to be Evangelized.
"All Things," to be taught Disciples.
"All the Days" the Lord's Presence Promised.

461. ## A Triple Glory of Christ.

Revelation i. 5.

The Faithful Witness; Incarnate on Earth—Past.
The First Begotten; Glorified in Heaven—Present.
The Prince of Kings; Reigning over all—Future.

462. ## A Threefold Exhortation.

Hebrews x. 19-24.

"Let us draw near" (Ver. 22)—Faith's Exercise.
"Let us hold fast" (Ver. 23)—Hope's Grasp.
"Let us consider" (Ver. 24)—Love's Labor.

463. ## Followers or "Imitators."

1 Thessalonians Chap. i. 11.

Followers of us and the Lord (Chap. i. 4)—Individual.
Followers of Churches of God (Chap. ii. 14)—Corporate.
The Gospel believed, produced the former (i. 4).
The Word received, effected the latter (ii. 13).

464. ## Three Stages in Christ's Path.

Philippians Chap. ii. 6-11.

From the Bosom of the Father to Bethlehem (Verses 6-7).
From the Manger to the Cross (Verses 7-8).
From the Grave to the Throne (Verses 9-11).

465.   Two Aspects of Christian Life.

A Man in Christ (2 Cor. xii. 1)—Standing.
Christ in Regenerate Man (2 Cor. xiii. 5)—State.

466.   Two Scenes in Luke's Gospel.

It opens with the Earthly Priest at the altar of incense on earth, and the people worshipping without in doubt and fear (Chap. i. 8-21).
It closes with the Great High Priest entering the Heavenly Temple, and His saints worshipping with great joy (Chap. xxiv. 50-53).

467.   Mansions or "Abodes"

In John, Chapter xiv.

Mansions awaiting Saints in God's Heaven (Ver. 2).
Mansions for God with Saints on earth (Ver. 23).
The word in the original is the same in both verses.

468.   Young Men of the Bible.

Patterns to Young Men in all ages.

Moses left all, in Faith (Heb. xi. 24).
Joseph endured all, in Hope (Gen. xlv. 5).
Jonathan surrendered all, in Love (1 Sam. xviii. 4).
Daniel triumphed over all, in Obedience (Dan. i. 6).

469.   Young Women of the Bible.

Bright Examples of Devotion.

Rebekah left all for Isaac (Gen. xxiv. 58).
Ruth found all in Bethlehem (Ruth ii. 12).
Esther risked all for her people (Esther iv. 16).

470. Two Characteristics of this Age.

The *Ascent* of the Son to the Throne (Chap. i.).
The *Descent* of the Spirit to the World (Chap. ii.).

471. Three Classes.

In 1 Corinthians x. 32.

"The Jew"; The National—Religious.
"The Gentile"; The Heathen—Idolatrous.
"The Church of God"; The Spiritual—Christians.

472. Eternal Life.

Promised by God (Titus i. 4)—Its Source.
Ever in Christ (John i. 4)—Its Spring.
Manifested by Christ (1 John i. 2)—Its Stream.
Given through Christ (Rom. vi. 23)—Its Channel.
Hid with Christ (Col. iii. 3)—Its Security.
Possessed by Believers (1 John v. 9)—A Present Enjoyment.
Hoped for in Fruition (Titus i. 2)—A Future Hope.

473. Lawlessness.

In its nature insubjection to God and His Word.

"Sin in Lawlessness" (1 John iii. 4, R.V.)
The Natural Condition of all (Rom. viii. 7; Job xi. 12).
Religious Profession Covers (Matt. xxiii. 7; 2 Tim. iii. 5).
Hated by the Lord Jesus (Heb. i. 9).
Redemption Delivers from it (Titus ii. 14).

474. Jesus Christ Our Shepherd.

The Good Shepherd (John x. 11)—Died to Save us.
The Great Shepherd (Heb. xiii. 20)—Lives to Guide us.
The Chief Shepherd (1 Pet. v. 3)—Comes to Glorify us.

475. Preaching in Acts x.

Preaching Peace through His Blood (ver. 36).
Proclaiming Forgiveness in His Name (ver. 44).
Announcing Judgment on the Impenitent (ver. 42).

476. Good Spiritual Condition.

Full of the Holy Ghost and Faith—Barnabas (Acts xi. 24).
Full of Faith and Power—Stephen (Acts vi. 8).
Full of Good Works and Almsdeeds—Dorcas (Acts ix. 36).

477. Seven Steps in Peter's Fall.

1. Doubts (Matt. xiv. 28, with xvi. 23).
2. Boasts (Mark xiv. 27-31, with 1 Cor. x. 12).
3. Sleeps (Mark xiv. 37, with Rom. xiii. 11).
4. Smites (John xviii. 10, with Luke xxii. 50).
5. Follows afar off (Luke xxii. 54).
6. Sits with the Ungodly (Luke xxii. 55).
7. Denies the Lord (Luke xxii. 57-62).

478. Seven Steps in Peter's Restoration.

1. The Lord's Prayer and Look (Luke xxii. 32-61).
2. Peter's Conviction, Tears, Repentance (Luke xxii. 61-62).
3. Hears and Hastens to the Sepulchre (John xx. 1-4).
4. Receives a message from the Lord (Mark xvi. 7).
5. Private Meeting with the Lord (Luke xxiv. 34).
6. Public Restoration to Service (John xxi. 15-17).
7. Boldly Testifies for Christ (Acts iii. 14).

BRIEFS FOR WORKERS

479. Willing and Wise.

A Willing Heart to give (Exod. xxxv. 5)—To God.
A Wise Heart to work (Exod. xxxv. 10)—For God.

480. Behind and Before.

"Forgetting"—the things that are behind.
"Forth-reaching"—to the glories that are before.

481. Lord and Master (Acts xxvii. 23).

"Whose I am"—Christ my Owner.
"Whom I serve"—Christ my Master.

482. Three Conditions of Soul.

"Cast Down" (2 Cor. vii. 6)—By Discouragement.
"Puffed Up" (Col. ii. 18)—In Pride.
"Pressing On" (Phil. iii. 14)—By Faith.

483. Credentials for Service.

Gift from God (Eph. iv. 8; 1 Pet. iv. 16).
Grace to use it to God (Eph. iv. 7; Rom. xii. 3).
Godliness to command it for God (1 Tim. iv. 7).

484. A Threefold Service (Jude 20, 21)

"BUILDING up yourselves (ver. 20)—The Word.
"PRAYING in the Holy Ghost" (ver. 20)—The Throne.
"LOOKING for the mercy of our Lord (ver. 21)—The Hope.

485.   A Triple Employment.

Pray Unceasingly (1 Thess. v. 17; Eph. vi. 18).
Praise Unflaggingly (Eph. v. 19-20; Heb. xiii. 15).
Preach Unweariedly (2 Tim. iv. 2; 1 Cor. xv. 58).

486.   Our Work in Three Aspects.

WORKERS for His Name (3 John 7).
WITNESSES for His Truth (Acts i. 8).
WATCHERS for His Coming (Mark xiii. 35).

487.   A Threefold Working.

The Lord working *for* us (John xvii. 4).
The Lord working *in* us (Heb. xiii. 21).
The Lord working *with* us (Mark xvi. 20).

488.   Our Stewardship.

A Steward of God (Titus i. 7)—A High Honor.
A Good Steward (1 Pet. iv. 10)—A Great Trust.
A Faithful Steward (1 Cor. iv. 2)—A Noble Aim.
A Wise Steward (Luke xii. 42)—A Discerning Mind.
An Unjust Steward (Luke xvi. 2)—A Selfish Motive.

489.   Badges of Christian Service.

Holiness (1 Thess. ii. 10, with Luke i. 75).
Humility (Acts xx. 19, with James iv. 6).
Hope (1 Cor. ix. 9, with James v. 7).

490.   Bugle Calls to Servants.

"Holding *faith* and a good conscience" (1 Tim. i. 19).
"Holding *fast* the faithful Word" (Titus i. 9).
"Holding *forth* the Word of Life" (Phil. ii. 12).

491. Fellowship in Service.

One Will (1 Cor. iv. 19; Jas. iv. 15).
One Walk (1 Cor. iv. 17; 2 Cor. xii. 18).
One Work (1 Cor. xvi. 10; xvi. 21).

492. Enoch, an Old Time Witness.

His faith in God (Heb. xi. 5).
His walk with God (Gen. v. 24).
His testimony for God (Jude 14).

493. Two Causes of Unfruitfulness.

"They had no root" (Matt. xiii. 6)—Christless.
"It lacked moisture" (Luke viii. 6)—Spiritless.

494. Walk and Work.

Walking with God (Gen. v. 24)—One Path.
Working with God (1 Sam. xiv. 45)—One Object.

495. Good Employment.

Always Praying (Phil. i. 4)—In the Spirit.
Always Rejoicing (2 Cor. vi. 10)—In the Lord.
Always Abounding (1 Cor. xv. 58)—In the Work.

496. The Gospeller.

Saved by the Gospel (2 Tim. i. 8-9)—Conversion.
Separated to the Gospel (Rom. i. 1)—Consecration.
Sent with the Gospel (Acts xiii. 4)—Commission.

497.   **Spiritual Outfit.**

Shod to walk (Deut. xxxiii. 25, with Eph. vi. 15).
Girded to Serve (Psa. xviii. 32, with John xiii. 4).
Armed to Fight (Eph. vi. 10, with 1 Tim. vi. 12).

498.   Paul's Preaching (Acts xx. 24-28).

The Gospel of the grace of God (Ver. 24)—The Message.
The Kingdom of God (Ver. 25)—The Object.
The Counsel of God (Ver. 27)—The Instrument.

499.   Watchwords of Service.

"HITHERTO hath the Lord helped us" (1 Sam. vii. 12).
"HENCEFORTH live . . . unto Him" (2 Cor. v. 13).

500.   "With Christ."

In Life (Eph. ii. 5).
In Suffering (2 Tim. ii. 17).
In Glory (John xvii. 34).